# THE TALMAGE STORY

James E Talmage

# THE

# TALMAGE

# STORY

## Life of James E. Talmage—
## Educator, Scientist, Apostle

### JOHN R. TALMAGE

BOOKCRAFT INC
SALT LAKE CITY, UTAH
1972

Library of Congress Catalog Card Number: 77-189831

1st Printing, 1972

LITHOGRAPHED IN U.S.A BY

PUBLISHERS PRESS
SALT LAKE CITY, UTAH

# Contents

# Illustrations

# Preface

Preparation and writing of this book have been, to me, a rare privilege. Going through the thirty volumes of James E. Talmage's personal journal gave me a wealth of detail, of insight into his personal life, and of just plain fascinating reading that were far more than ample reward for any effort I may have expended. Many incidents which took place during my own lifetime came alive again as I read Father's written accounts, and it was almost (but never, of course, quite) like having him back for a brief visit.

Most of the material in this book is based on the record of James E. Talmage's own journals. Some things here, however, were not recorded in the journals, but were recorded elsewhere or were told to me, or to other members of the family, by Father himself. I have tried to avoid, or at least to minimize, the use of speculation or imagination on my own part.

I had hoped to write this book much earlier, but I found that the problems, duties, and frequent interruptions involved in raising a family were too numerous to permit sustained creative effort at home in evenings and over weekends. Having to earn a living, eventually I took the only practical course left open and established a writing schedule between 4:30 and 6:30 A.M., when I could work uninterrupted. I feel that in a way this was peculiarly fitting and that perhaps it helped my writing, as it was typical of Father's own approach to problems of this sort. I regret to say that it is all too untypical of my own normal approach.

I wish to express special appreciation to my wife, Virginia, both for her understanding and forbearance and for doing the finished typing of the manuscript for the book.

My sincere wish is that I have managed to bring out for those who know James E. Talmage only through his writings, some feeling of the warmth and humanity, the love and understanding of the man whom hundreds of thousands know as the author of *Jesus the Christ* and *The Articles of Faith* and whom I knew as the most wonderful of fathers.

JOHN R. TALMAGE

# Boyhood in England

James Edward Talmage, whose voice and pen were to be counted among the most eloquent champions of The Church of Jesus Christ of Latter-day Saints, was born September 21, 1862, a Sunday, in the little town of Hungerford, Berkshire, England, to James Joyce and Susannah Preater Talmage. He was the eldest son and eldest surviving child of a family which eventually numbered eleven children. One child, a daughter named Patience, had been born earlier and had died at the age of two years.

At the time of the birth of James E., his parents were managing the Bell Hotel in Hungerford and the child was born at that hostelry and spent the first two years of his life there. Then, probably because a hotel was a difficult and in many obvious ways undesirable place in which to rear a child, young James was taken by his paternal grandfather to live with him at his home in Ramsbury, a village some five miles from Hungerford, but across the county line in Wiltshire. Young James spent all of the next three years with his grandfather "attending infant school at different times," and the child developed a deep attachment to the grandfather which remained a major influence throughout his life. In later years he delighted in telling his own children and grandchildren stories of Grandfather Talmage, stories of formal and informal lessons taught and learned, of occasional stern admonitions, of joyous outings in pursuit of fish in the canal that ran between Hungerford and Ramsbury or of waterfowl and small game in the marshes and fields; and through them all ran always the vibrant feeling of loving remembrance that invariably lights the eye and warms the voice of one speaking of someone unusually close and deeply loved, who has exerted a major influence for good on the speaker's life.

James Talmage, the grandfather, was by all accounts a man of strong character, lively emotions, and vigorously-held opinions who was well worth knowing. Born in 1799, he was in the full vigor of manhood when the Latter-day Saint missionaries first came to Ramsbury. As a natural leader of the young—and impulsive—set, he was in the forefront of the anti-Mormon element and was prepared to give the uninvited preachers a violent send-off from the community when they held their first public meeting and began to tell the story of Mormonism in the Wiltshire village. However, something in the manner of the missionaries, probably their quiet dignity in the face of threatened violence and their forthright fearlessness without bravado, appealed to the Briton's strong sense of fair play.

Whatever it was, James Talmage found himself—somewhat to his own mystification, he related later—helping the Mormon Elders to escape when local feelings erupted into full mob violence, instead of leading the tar-and-feather-'em, ride-'em-out-of-town-on-a-rail element into action as he had fully intended to do.

At considerable risk to himself, for feelings were running high in the mob, young Talmage managed to help the missionaries elude their pursuers and to hide them in his own home until the emotional storm in the community blew over. There were some tense moments, as when the mob trailed the fugitives to the Talmage door and milled about, loudly threatening to tear the house down, while the young master hid the Elders in a closet and somehow managed to convince the mob that the trail they were following led elsewhere.

In the end, the ruse was successful, the angry mob drifted away, and the Mormon Elders were spared severe indignities and discomfort, if not worse. The author of their deliverance still felt only that he had responded to an appeal to his sense of fair play, and he fully intended to send the fugitives packing as soon as the coast was clear and they had had a chance to eat a little food which his wife prepared for them.

Something, however, led him to listen to what the missionaries had to say, when they began to expound their Gospel message as soon as they had fittingly voiced their thanks for the timely help they had received. In spite of himself, the Englishman was impressed, and soon he was actively seeking further enlightenment instead of having it thrust upon him. Before long, he had become a full-scale investigator of Mormonism, in time was convinced of the truth of the message, and eventually was baptized into the Church.

In due time, his own family went into the waters of baptism, and so it happened that James E. Talmage, the grandson, although coming into the world at a time and place where Mormonism was scarcely known, was born as virtually a third-generation member of the Church.[1]

Young James E.'s own baptism, performed by his father, did not take place at the customary age of eight years, and actually was delayed until he was nearing his eleventh birthday, various considerations having caused the delay. But the occasion, when it did finally arrive, was one that was never forgotten by any of those who were present.

In the spring of 1873, when James was in his eleventh year, he suffered an illness that became so critical that his life appeared imminently threatened. His father, in deep parental despair, associated the illness with the fact that the boy's baptism had been so long delayed. Father Talmage made a solemn covenant with the Lord that, if his boy's life should be spared, he would be baptized as soon as possible after his recovery. The boy did recover, and arrangements for the baptism were promptly made.

Due to opposition which at times "threatened persecution" of Latter-day Saints in the community, baptisms were

[1]There is some confusion about exact dates of baptism of the first and second generations of the Talmage family to come into the Church. Records were sketchily kept in those early days in the overseas missions, and in keeping with the then-current custom the family was re-baptized after reaching Utah. There is one reference in James E. Talmage's journal to recollections of Church of England services "before Father was baptized into the Church," so there was apparently a considerable interval between the time of the baptism of Grandfather Talmage and that of his son, James Joyce, father of James Edward. There is no question, however, that James E. was the third generation of his immediate line to embrace the Gospel and that he was reared in accordance with Church tenets.

performed at night. James' baptism was set for the night of June 15, 1873, in a millrace paralleling the Kennet River, only a short distance from the cottage the Talmage family was occupying in Eddington, a suburb of Hungerford. A young girl of the Hungerford Branch of the Church, Ellen Gilbert (later Mrs. Andrew L. Hyer, wife of the bishop of the Lewiston, Idaho, First Ward), was to be baptized on the same occasion.

When the hour appointed for the ordinances approached, Father Talmage and Ellen's brother Elijah, a deacon in the branch, left the Talmage cottage where the little baptismal party had assembled, and carefully reconnoitered the neighborhood. No one appeared to be abroad, and the Latter-day Saint group quickly proceeded to the waterside.

Father Talmage stepped into the stream and held out his hand for young James. At that moment, James later related, "we were horror-stricken by such a combined scream, howl, shriek, yell—I know not how to describe the noise— as none of us had ever heard before." It seemed to be "a combination of every fiendish ejaculation that we could conceive of," and to his dying day James never forgot "how I trembled at the awful manifestation, which had about it the sharpness of a thunderclap followed by an angry roll."

"Father asked me if I was too frightened to be baptized, and I answered by directly stepping into the water," James recalled. "The unearthly noise ceased the instant I stepped into the water."

Both his baptism and Ellen Gilbert's immediately afterward were performed without further unusual incident.

James rarely spoke of this peculiar experience, and even in his private journal he refrained from drawing any specific conclusion. Certain facts, however, speak for themselves:

The diabolical noise was heard by every member of the baptismal party, but by no one else. A cautious round of inquiry the next day failed to turn up any hint that anyone else in the area had heard an unusual disturbance during the

James Joyce Talmage and Susannah Preater Talmage, parents of James E. Talmage. Both family lines were settled in the area near London in the counties of Berkshire and Wiltshire.

night. The horrifying screaming began as the candidates for baptism approached the water, and ceased abruptly when young James stepped into the millrace so that the ordinance could be performed.

Before reaching the age when he was baptized into the Church, young James had passed through a number of experiences of significance in his life.

At the age of five years, having spent three full years in his grandfather's care in Ramsbury, the youngster returned to live with his parents in Hungerford, "attending school at irregular intervals for a period of three years," as he notes in his journal; this, together with the earlier note concerning his occasional attendance at the "infant school" in Ramsbury, offering somewhat surprising insight into the early age at which British children began their educational training in the late 1860's.

One of the tragedies of James' life, which undoubtedly had a profound influence on shaping his whole outlook, occurred when the boy was less than a month past his eleventh birthday. In his personal journal, which he began to write about four years later and continued almost to the day of his death, young James set down a brief summary of the early years of his life. The following stark account contains, in the words of a boy of fifteen, the memory of the most terrible event he had experienced:

> On October 10, 1873, while working after nightfall—a very dark night—a fearful accident occurred. My brother Albert, then about six years of age, came quietly towards me as I was still working with a digging fork in my hands; he gave no notice of his approach and until he screamed I had not an idea he was near me; then to my horror I discovered that while in the act of pitching with the fork I had struck him with the tool, one grain piercing the ball of his left eye. This organ was finally entirely removed, though not before the right eye had become sympathetically affected and he was almost absolutely blind, being only enabled to distinguish very bright colors, and then only when within a few inches of the eye. . . . True, "evils must come, but woe unto them by whom they come." I need say nothing in

regard to my feelings and reflections at this mishap; but that my relief lies in the promise pronounced on him by the priesthood of God that he shall recover.

The inner turmoil, the soul-searing anguish, the sheer nightmarish horror that tore at the heart of the boy who had innocently caused the blinding of a dearly loved younger brother may be imagined; although it is probable that the possessor of the most vivid imagination could not—unless its owner had undergone some comparably traumatic experience —picture a fraction of the torment in the boy's mind.

More than any other event, or series of events, this awful occurrence may account for the deep, almost fanatical dedication to work, to Church duties and to all the serious adult responsibilities that marked the life of young James E. Talmage from that terrible day forward. Reading his journal, or hearing his contemporaries talk about him, one has difficulty in realizing that the James Talmage of the mid-1870's was a teen-age youth. Indeed, it is sometimes difficult to imagine his having had a boyhood at all. Only occasionally does a glimmer of boyish interest and enthusiasm for boyish things peep through, almost between the lines, as it were, of his personal journal. And then, the revealing insights are most likely to come in passing mention of nostalgic memories, years afterward.

In later, adult years, when he returned to England to attend the meetings of world-renowned scientific societies and found time to revisit the scenes of his childhood, Dr. Talmage almost always made at least one excursion to the canal where he had fished as a boy. In June, 1891, on the occasion of his first return to Britain and to his boyhood home, he wrote:

> Among other desires, I have longed to go a-fishing again, *as I used to do,* in the Canal that passes through the town. Today, Elder Prye and myself prepared for this species of recreation. I fully realized the wish expressed above—I fished *as I used to do,* staying hour after hour at the water side, and catching nothing.

Other fishing-pole-in-hand returns to boyhood were more productive, but all of them show the fond memories of this sport which never faded with the years but which were not so much as hinted at in contemporary journal entries.

On May 8, 1874, young James passed an examination of the Oxford Diocesan Association and was admitted to the Hungerford National School. There is evidence that he did well scholastically, but in later visits to Hungerford Dr. Talmage always referred to the National School as "the place where I received so many thrashings" or in some similar phrase indicating frequent and severe chastisements by his schoolmaster, a Mr. James Newhook.

The truth is that the boy was an excellent scholar, but that he clashed frequently with his schoolmaster over questions of religion. Mr. Newhook took a dim view of Latter-day Saints and of Mormon doctrine, and apparently felt no delicate reservations about expressing himself on the subject openly and forcefully in the classroom. His young pupil possessed a notable "temper" and an unswerving determination to stand up for what he believed to be right, even at the expense of considerable physical suffering, "canings" being an accepted school disciplinary measure, to be administered at the discretion of the schoolmaster.

On the occasions of his later visits to Hungerford, Dr. Talmage never failed to call on Mr. Newhook and the latter received him in his home with enthusiasm, taking great pride in the scientific achievements of his erstwhile pupil, but never ceasing to marvel that anything good could have come from one who embraced Mormonism and emigrated to far-off Utah.

Schooling was interrupted for a time in 1874 when the young scholar withdrew from classes to accompany Grandfather Talmage on a tour through Berkshire and Hampshire, and again shortly after their return home when the old gentleman (he was now in his seventy-fifth year) took seriously ill. Young James returned to Ramsbury and solicitously nursed his grandfather through four weeks of illness of increasing severity, at the end of which the old gentleman died. Death came on July 16, 1874.

"Having been closely attached to him," young James wrote in his journal, "his death affected me severely; and the more so as I had never before lost a near relative to my knowledge." He continued:

> I began to reflect seriously on his actions as brought up by memory, to note them very closely and at length to meditate on his present lot; fully knowing he died in the possession of the priesthood and a firm belief and faith in The Church of Jesus Christ of Latter-day Saints. One night while meditating in this manner I received a very curious dream concerning him (the details are probably immaterial) which had the effect of so firmly imprinting on my mind the conviction that his lot was "all right" that not the slightest doubt in that respect has ever been entertained.

This passage is typical of the boy's confiding in his journal at this age, particularly the parenthetical note that "the details [of the dream] are probably immaterial." He was unusually reticent about setting down details of his deeply personal thoughts and feelings. This is unfortunate from the point of view of one reading his journal today, but this rarely-broken habit gives his journal an extraordinarily strong flavor of objectivity that has its own special value.

Even before the death of Grandfather Talmage the family had been thinking seriously of emigrating to Utah, and when the old man passed away they proceeded to carry the plans into action. Father Talmage ended his connection with the Bell Hotel in Hungerford and moved his family into the family home in Ramsbury until it could be satisfactorily disposed of.

Once that was done, they enrolled as Mormon emigrants and on May 22, 1876, left their home in Ramsbury. Two days later, in Liverpool, the family boarded a ship to cross the Atlantic as the first leg on their trip to Zion, the dreamed-of gathering place of the Saints.

# To America

The ocean trip aboard the SS *Nevada* of the old Gurion line must have been an experience of wondrous excitement for the boy of thirteen who was venturing outside his native island-country for the first time, but James' only journal mention of the ocean crossing is astonishingly brief, as is the description of the railway trip across the continent.

> Set sail on board the Steamship "Nevada" of Gurion Line of Steamers from Liverpool May 24, 1876. The acting president of our company was "John Woodhouse," a returning missionary. Voyage lasted twelve days, during which one severe storm was experienced, though on the whole a pleasant voyage must be chronicled. June 5, 1876 landed in good health at Castle Gardens, New York, U.S. America, and continuing our journey we started June 6 on board cars and arrived in Salt Lake City, Utah, June 14, 1876, where we remained one week. June 21 we left for Provo City, Utah County, where my father purchased a house and lot and we made our home.

Thus condensed is the boy's account of what must have been the great adventure of his life to that time. Some of the explanation for the brevity of the account lies in the fact that it is a part of the summary of his life to date when he began to keep a personal journal in December, 1879. But it is regrettable that he did not set down the details of his impressions of the trip, of the new land, and its customs and way of life as he did, for instance, on the occasion of his first return to his native England and on other special occasions throughout his life.

Just two months after arriving in Provo, James enrolled in the grammar department of Brigham Young Academy and first came in contact with a man who was to exert a lasting influence on his life, the late great educator Dr. Karl G. Maeser.

With his heavy beard, excitable temperament, comic-opera German accent and nervous mannerisms of the absent-minded professor, Dr. Maeser was, underneath, a great teacher. He possessed, to an extraordinary degree, the ability to kindle in his students the burning desire for knowledge. A profound scholar himself, he had the missionary zeal of the born teacher who cannot rest until he has tried to impart to others the joy which he has found in learning.

The meeting of the elderly German professor and the intense, dedicated English boy was fateful. The youth's thirst for knowledge, already noteworthy, became a consuming fire which, together with his love of the Gospel and unswerving dedication to Church duties, remained the driving force behind his actions throughout his life. The old professor also bene-fitted greatly from the association, finding in his young pro-tegé an invaluable helper in the tremendous task he had undertaken, to spread the light of learning in a pioneer com-munity where the accepted tools and facilities of education were woefully scarce and where the teacher must depend on his ingenuity and resourcefulness almost as much as on his store of formally-acquired knowledge.

After enrolling at BYA, James had about three terms, some thirty weeks, of uninterrupted schooling—something pre-cious for the boy whose school attendance had been so fre-quently interrupted in England—before he was forced to with-draw for a time to help his father with the heavy work of establishing a farm. He returned to classes in August, 1877, and was given the responsibility of recorder of the Inter-mediate Department of the Academy, but he had to resign that position and again interrupt his own schooling when he suffered a severe attack of what was then called "brain fever," which confined him to his bed for some two months. This was one of the first of many indications, lasting throughout his life, of a tendency to overwork to the point of exhaustion and severe physical illness.

If he suspected that overwork was the reason for his sickness, he managed to disregard the implication completely. On returning to school in January, 1878, he accepted the responsibilities—in addition to the normal ones imposed by his own course of study—of secretary of the faculty and academy librarian and the additional extra-curricular and off-campus posts of librarian of the academy's "Polysophical Society," secretary and librarian of the Provo Third Ward Sunday School and secretary of the Mutual Improvement Association of the same ward. After six months, this heavy schedule was obviously threatening his health and he was forced to resign the ward positions, but he continued his special assignments at the Academy and his regular course of studies (plus courses in Latin and German from the advanced section of the institution) until June 15, 1879, when, he wrote in his journal, "I enrolled my name as one of a corps of twelve candidates for Normal Diplomas."

"Theoretical examinations," he further noted, "lasted five days."

At the end of those five days, James emerged with an official grade of "99 per cent in efficiency and 100 per cent in standing." In addition, Dr. Maeser presented him with a graduating certificate of 100 per cent efficiency for "composition," and he was named to "deliver an address in the public hall in behalf of the corps of graduates"—what today would be called valedictorian of the class, albeit of a class of twelve.

Following graduation he devoted most of the summer to helping on the farm, but returned to the Academy in August, both to pursue his own education in more advanced areas and also as a part-time member of the faculty.

# The Young Teacher

James E. Talmage began his teaching career at Brigham Young Academy on August 21, 1879, exactly one month before his seventeenth birthday. The date is established beyond any question, but one reading the teen-ager's journal and following his activities through this medium has repeatedly to remind himself that the youth was in very fact a boy and not a mature man. The written words seem to have come from the pen of one much older than seventeen.

He noted in his journal entry for August 21 that he "entered the B.Y. Academy on a nominal salary as teacher of Intermediate and some Academic branches, and continued my own study of Latin and natural sciences."

The "nominal salary" appears to have been about $1.25 a week. The list of subjects taught is not detailed in the journal, but it definitely included academic grammar, academic penmanship, and drawing; and before the end of the school term there were added to his teaching responsibilities classes in physiology, Latin reading, and phonography—the latter being the original Pitman shorthand—all this without any increase in salary.

The course in shorthand proved so popular that within a month the young instructor was conducting an additional class, an hour earlier than the opening of the regular school program, to accommodate those desirous of taking the course but whose regular schedule of hours was filled. The following school year, three classes in phonography were offered to meet the demand, and it is interesting to note that in later years when James was enrolled in eastern universities he conducted classes in phonography for the townspeople which drew most enthusiastic response. This skill in shorthand also brought the young teacher a great deal of extra work, as he was much in demand to report school, Church and community events in a day when shorthand reporters were a rarity.

In his first year as a teacher, James had a number of duties in addition to those of actual classroom instruction and to those frequent but irregular demands on his services as a public reporter. Included in these duties were the posts of secretary to the faculty (again making use of his shorthand skill), curator of the Academy museum and laboratory, school librarian, and chairman of the Scientific Section of the Academy's Polysophical Society, which was the principal cultural-scientific-social extra-curricular activity on the campus.

All in all, there appears little doubt that the young man of seventeen fully earned his $1.25 a week.

A year later, when the Academy's youngest teacher had been accorded two salary increases and was making $75 per school term, his workload had been enlarged accordingly. His teaching schedule included classes in philosophy, chemistry, geology, Latin reading, phonography, academic penmanship, and academic grammar.

Those were other times with other customs, and pay in any line of work was astonishingly low by today's standards. It is also true that Brigham Young Academy's youngest teacher in the early 1880's was very young indeed. Nevertheless, the stipend was small even by the standards of the day and taking into account all special conditions, and James had to do some vigorous wrestling with his innermost feelings before he could accept conditions at which his instincts rebelled.

When first offered the "raise" to $75 a term, he wrote in his journal:

> I decided at once that I could not accept the offer. Consulted father and also Brother Maeser before giving an answer. Bro. M. showed me that the Academy is a missionary institution, and as I had become connected with it I should keep on. Also that the

almost to the opening of the fall term at Brigham Young Academy.

This was the first of many trips around the state and surrounding territory which, over the years, provided James E. Talmage with an unusually wide circle of friends and acquaintances, but on this maiden excursion he felt very much alone and was keenly aware of the contrast presented by his travelling companions, who had friends of long standing in every community they visited.

"Found that it is well to have plenty of friends while travelling, never was in the northern settlements before, hence have no acquaintances; expect to make some before leaving, however," he wrote in his journal on July 3. A boy's feeling of loneliness is clearly discernible in the terse observation, and at a time when travellers "put up" with hospitable families along the way rather than in public accommodations (which rarely existed in the smaller communities) there was a very practical consideration involved. However, the expressed intention to make friends and acquaintances before leaving each town or settlement was fulfilled and there is no further comment in this vein; instead there are frequent and sincere entries expressing deep appreciation for the openhearted hospitality showered on him by people who had been total strangers.

Schools throughout the "northern territory" were visited and the youngest member of the inspection party made copious notes which he recorded in his journal, such as "perhaps I may be able to direct my own course advantageously—if I adopt the teacher's profession."

He meticulously noted such detail as the light falling from the right instead of from the left in one classroom, the placing of the heating apparatus, and the positioning of the blackboard. Comments were made on the degree of preparation and effectiveness of presentation of various teachers, and the conduct of devotional exercises. Observations were sometimes critical, sometimes warmly commendatory, but always objective.

A new type of experience awaited the party at Soda Springs, Idaho, where they were invited to stay with a Brother Horsley. Returning from a visit to the springs from which the town takes its name ("a fine locality for the naturalist, especially the chemist and geologist"), they found themselves confronted with a real emergency. Their host's son Herbert had accidentally shot himself. The large-calibre bullet had entered his right thigh, close to the groin, and had taken a downward course and finally lodged against the knee cap. The mishap had occurred when the young man was alone, ten miles from home, and he had to drive a team of horses that distance. When he arrived at the house, his father was absent; and his mother and sisters were doing what little they could to ease the pain when the visitors returned from the springs.

Thereupon the youngest member of the school inspection group disclosed an ability to take charge and act decisively in the face of an emergency. James had had no formal training in medicine, but his own father had acted as the informal village doctor in England in days when physicians and surgeons with accredited degrees were rarities, and the boy must have learned a good deal by assisting his father at various times. His own diligent investigations into all branches of the natural sciences also had given him considerable knowledge of human anatomy.

James promptly took over, washing the wound while others hastened to summon the injured man's father.

When Brother Horsley, Senior, returned and was consulted, "no surgeon being at hand (as James recorded in his journal), and the wound being a dangerous one, the knee swelling up very rapidly, at the express request of his parents and by the counsel of Brother Maeser, I attempted to extract the bullet." The journal continues:

> By the help of God, I succeeded with no apparent serious consequences. Brother Moench [another member of the visiting group] then assisted me and we endeavored to clean the wound and strap up the cut with plaster. The wound now gave little pain and the patient soon slept. I sat up during the night, and

knowing that sleep was the chief requisite, the young man being exhausted by pain and loss of blood; endeavored to keep him sleeping by applying cold water to the wound whenever it became excessively hot. In the morning, no sign of inflammation was apparent.

The patient, it was subsequently learned, recovered rapidly and completely.

The school inspection trip continued through the Idaho settlements and finally returned to Utah and was declared officially ended on September 9 at Ogden.

Young James Talmage found, however, that the return home was still to be delayed. Brother Maeser informed him that he would be expected to teach all classes in chemistry at Brigham Young Academy the ensuing school year and "acting under the counsel of Brother Maeser and with the sanction of President John Taylor," he decided to remain in Ogden for "two weeks' observations from experiments by Mr. Thomas Hadley, an English graduate in chemistry." The Academy "kindly advanced me the means on my salary for next year," to buy the necessary chemicals and to pay for room and board at the Hadley home.

After a period of intensive study, interrupted long enough to comply with a request that he deliver a lecture before the Ogden (Mutual) Improvement Associations, a talk which drew a large audience and considerable favorable comment in the press, the young man of not quite eighteen years hastened back to Provo just in time for the opening of the new school year. He noted, a little wistfully, in his journal: "Indeed, very little vacation has fallen to my share this year."

# CHAPTER FOUR

# Plans for College

With the beginning of the 1880-81 school year, young James E. Talmage found that vacation and recreational pursuits were less likely than ever to "fall to his share" as his duties—both regular and extra-curricular—increased still further, as also did his determination to advance his own education.

It has already been noted that he received his second advance in salary, to the glittering sum of $75 per school term, at the beginning of the new school year, and that his teaching load was increased accordingly. Very briefly, it appeared that he might be relieved of some of the extra workload, when he was unexpectedly notified of his release from the position of secretary of the faculty; but the release was coupled to a new appointment to the position of deputy treasurer of the institution. This new duty was to take a great deal of time and effort, and to cost him considerable mental anguish and some hard cash, which he could ill spare, as time went by. Handling cash and keeping cash accounts were contrary both to his inclination and his talents, and invariably he would find small discrepancies when the books were balanced at the end of each school term, discrepancies which he made up from his own pocket. While the amounts were comparatively small, they were nevertheless severely felt by one whose means were as tightly stretched as were his, and it was with a feeling of enormous relief that he was finally, after seven school terms of service, able to obtain acceptance of his repeatedly offered resignation from the position.

Finances presented a continuing problem to the young teacher. While in no wise ambitious to become wealthy, he was understandably concerned with laying something aside for his future in life. Later in the school year, when the question of salary was again broached with the academy authorities and he was again counselled by Brother Maeser to be content to proceed slowly and to regard his calling largely as one of missionary labor, he reflected:

> I have no desire to get rich; that is not my object at all, but I must sustain myself properly. Most boys of my age have gathered around them property of some kind, but I have neglected all, using all my energies to continue at school. . . . I can see plainly that I will not be enabled to save the least means for a start in life [on the BYA salary scale]. In fact, I cannot see my way clear for my future course. Never mind, I trustingly pass on! Decided that as my duty certainly demanded me to make somewhat of a return to my parents for their endeavors to assist me in attending school, I would pay Father $40 per term out of the $100 I receive.

A year later, when he was advanced to $600 per school year, he again wrestled with his soul, but philosophically decided: "I believe I'm destined to remain poor; well, I never desired to be rich." Then he added a little wistfully, "but when the need for some book or piece of [scientific] apparatus harasses me I often wish to strike a mine with just enough wealth to sustain me."

Assuming responsibility for teaching all of the courses in science and most "philological" (in its now-obsolete meaning of "classical scholarship") branches of study at the Academy, James felt the responsibility keenly. He rejoiced in the fact that his teaching obligations required him to do extensive research; in fact, he counted this a credit toward making up the deficit in monetary remuneration for his work at the Academy.

"I am teaching all higher scientific or philological branches, in order to do which I am necessitated to work up on the subjects myself, thereby opening up to me a field of research which is almost as beneficial as regularly attending school," he philosophized on one of the occasions when he was trying to reconcile himself to his low salary. Nevertheless, he was keenly aware of his deficiencies in formal qualifications for the academic position he held and constantly worked to overcome them.

He firmly resolved to map out each day's classroom lectures in advance, and in minute detail in order to "avoid superficiality" and to make certain he was master of the subject of each lecture. He closely adhered to this self-imposed requirement, even though it reduced the hours available for sleeping to a maximum of four or five a night—thereby beginning the establishment of a sleep (or perhaps it is better described as a sleep-*less*) pattern that led to a chronic insomnia which plagued him sorely through the remainder of his life.

"My labors will be arduous at the Academy," he reflected, "but I must scarcely expect to spend many more such peaceful seasons, so I shall endeavor to make the best of this one. I mean by 'peaceful seasons' that opportunities for study and research will not last long. I may be sent on a mission before another winter or my occupation may be varied to admit of but little time for private study."

The schedule the young man evolved to "make the best of this peaceful season" provided for experimental work in the laboratory from the end of the school day until 10 P.M. He noted that "this would not amount to more than three hours per night as my incidental work [at the Academy] would occupy my time until after supper. My sleeping hours will be from 10 P.M. to 4:30 A.M. and my study at home from that time until school time. I feel to chide myself on not grasping opportunities for work in the laboratory, etc., as they cannot last forever."

What this planned schedule failed to take into account was the frequent demands on the young instructor's time to deliver talks and lectures, demands that were almost invariably met by taking the necessary time from the already-limited hours budgeted for sleep.

At the close of the 1880-81 academic year, James was busy as a faculty member of the Academy Examining Board, and still busier as a candidate for special examinations as a "teacher of natural sciences." He confided to his journal:

> In this instance the obtaining of a diploma is *per se* a secondary consideration. I have detected a feeling among some, my acquaintances generally, that I am not competent to teach the branches I attempt. My diploma will certainly confer on me greater authority and evoke a feeling of such among the students. In making this statement, I speak on principle and not from selfish or egotistical feeling.

The precise effect on the critics is not recorded, but it was no doubt significant, for the young teacher emerged from his series of examinations before Professor Maeser, the noted educator whose training had been obtained under the rigorous German educational standards, with an impressive record: "Natural philosophy, 100% in theoretical, 98% in practical; astronomy, 100% theoretical, 95% practical; chemistry, 100%* theoretical, 100% practical; geology, 100%* theoretical, 100% practical; human physiology, 100% theoretical, 95% practical; zoology, 100% theoretical, 99% practical; botany, 100%* theoretical, 100% practical"—the asterisks alongside certain of the grades indicating the examiner's notation "with excellence."

With another very full work-year behind him at the close of the examination period in June, 1881, the young man looked forward to a more restful interlude, although his definition of "rest" might not fully agree with that of most young people. His program for the summer vacation was a horse-and-wagon trip around the county to study geological formations and to collect specimens.

His plans were largely doomed to disappointment, although he did manage to make a start at carrying them out. Accompanied by Reinhardt Maeser, son of the professor, and Simon P. Eggertson, he set out the day following the close of the school term for a tour of the mining camps south and west of Utah Lake. Despite problems with a horse that strayed away one night and eventually turned up lame, the three young men made an enjoyable and successful field trip, were well received in the camps where they were allowed to inspect various mining operations, and returned to Provo six days after setting out with a substantial store of mineral specimens.

Before another excursion could be so much as mapped out, however, word came from Church headquarters in Salt Lake that Professor Maeser and young James Talmage were called to make a tour to inspect the schools in the southern part of the state, a trip comparable to the one they had made through the northern settlements the previous summer. The inspection tour was in many ways a close parallel to the earlier one, but the actual travel was more rugged. The railroad ended at Milford and travel beyond that point was by horse-drawn (or occasionally mule-drawn) wagon. There were some long hauls between settlements, considerable camping out, and the notorious summer heat of Utah's Dixie, but the travelers made very little complaint about physical conditions, save in a few instances where the local water supply upset their digestion.

The inspection trip lasted nearly seven weeks and was filled to overflowing with meetings, conferences and interviews. It appears to have fulfilled its purpose, and drawn high praise for its participants from many sources, including the First Presidency of the Church; which led young James to some critical self-analysis in the privacy of his journal. On August 22, the day he returned home, he wrote:

> The authorities have often spoken of my age and diligent labors in public and even President Woodruff tonight was not an exception, but I see one thing, that this very circumstance imposes on me an onerous duty—to keep opinion of self down. . . . Some think me *conceited,* but I think they are those that know me but little. I am not so; indeed, I am impetuous, rushing, energetic, and these traits are often taken for self-conceit.

The course of the 1881-82 school year generally followed the pattern of those immediately preceding it, the pattern being one of overcrowded hours and periodic additions to a schedule already more than full.

Some scientific apparatus had been purchased by the Academy and had been delivered while the teacher was away on the summer inspection trip, a fact that was noted with intense satisfaction; but the apparatus required a great deal of time-consuming labor to put it in proper condition for classroom and laboratory use, and to keep it in usable condition through the school year.

The problems of poor quality or makeshift apparatus— or of complete lack of suitable apparatus—were a constant source of irritation to the young teacher. The Academy operated on a very limited budget and could provide only a small part of what he felt was needed. He strained his personal resources, such as they were, to the limit and perhaps beyond, without much practical effect. His soul was filled with constant longing, not for personal wealth, but for the proper tools of learning and of teaching.

One of the particular problems which he faced was the lack of interest—or, often, active hostility—toward science *per se*. In the deeply religious, largely uneducated community, science was generally viewed with suspicion and mistrust. This was not the attitude of the Academy administration, of course, nor of the General Authorities of the Church, who strongly encouraged the teaching of natural sciences, but the attitude was present in a large part of the student body and a factor to be reckoned with.

"Science is to many people a revolting name," James noted in December, 1881. With the instinct of the born teacher for visual aids and dramatic presentation of basic facts, he constantly sought ways and means to give his scientific lectures more popular appeal.

One of the most effective dramatizations was entirely unplanned. On December 7, 1881, a scheduled lecture on the composition of water was being delivered before the Scientific Section of BYA's Polysophical Society. It was to be dramatically illustrated by a controlled explosion of very small amounts of oxygen and hydrogen, to synthesize $H_2O$ before the eyes of the onlookers. The dramatic effect exceeded all plans and expectations.

The glass cylinder in which the "controlled" explosion was taking place "burst with such a concussion as to extinguish all lamps in the room excepting those held in the chandeliers."

Near-panic ensued, but the lecturer managed to restore order in a short time. Injuries, very fortunately, were few and minor. One young lady was struck in the forehead by a small fragment of flying glass. In recording the incident, James noted:

> When she discovered traces of blood, she fainted very nicely, and I changed at once my occupation from that of a public lecturer to an attendant physician. She recovered, however, when 'twas found that the large amounts of blood filling the bowl from which I was bathing her head came from my own hand. Two pieces of glass had struck the index finger of my right hand, one fragment burying itself in the knuckle joint.

Another young lady received a piece of flying glass which pierced her clothing and inflicted "a severe gash" on her shoulder. Four or five more "were robbed of traces of skin" and all in the audience "were severely scared."

As soon as the wounded had been properly treated, James, with a showman's instinct, quickly returned to the platform to complete the lecture, which action "did much to lessen the fear of the audience." The young lecturer chided himself for allowing what might have been a much more serious accident, especially for not insisting that the audience remain at the extreme rear of the lecture room.

"Although I had twice sent them back, whenever I commenced a new experiment as many as possibly could crowded around," he said, describing not only this particular audience but all audiences from time immemorial. The dry spoken word may leave listeners somnolently in their seats, but the first promise of exciting action brings them scurrying front and center.

There were dire predictions that the frightening accident would douse completely the flickering interest in scientific lectures, but James Talmage believed that the psychological effect would be quite opposite, and events proved him right. Just one week later, the next scheduled lecture before the Scientific Section was so well attended as to put standing room at a premium "and the rostrum upon which I had placed my apparatus was literally besieged." From that time on, attendance at lectures on science continued high, as students turned out with a delicious thrill of half-scared, half-hoping anticipation of another spectacular explosion. In this hope they were occasionally rewarded, although greater care was taken in the future to prevent injury to spectators.

While recognizing the dramatic appeal of the unexpected explosion and at the same time wisely taking precautions against a dangerous repetition, the young teacher earnestly strove to find visual aids and techniques that would fire audience-interest without adding any element of danger. One of the most longed-for of these was a "stereopticon," or optical lantern.

After despairing of prevailing on the Academy authorities to purchase the lantern (the authorities were not unsympathetic to the idea and its potentialities, but merely short of funds) James and George Coray, a friend on the BYA faculty, conceived the idea of themselves purchasing an optical lantern, using it in their school classes and also to illustrate a series of public lectures for which they proposed to charge modest admission fees until they had recovered their investment. The plan proved to be an artistic success but a financial failure.

Despite numerous problems—among them, the difficulty of obtaining just the right kind of slides, and technical harassments such as the tendency of a small mica "window" to break and the extreme difficulty of securing replacement parts—the optical lantern was a wonderful help in presenting scientific lectures, and the interest among BYA students showed a marked increase. The plan to give public lectures for a fee in order to regain the investment, however, did not materialize and the cost of the stereopticon, slides, and replacement parts ended up as a personal contribution by the young men to the cause of scientific education. Furthermore, James Talmage eventually bought out George Coray at the latter's request and thus assumed the entire financial burden, which was a heavy one in view of his severely limited resources.

Acquisition of the stereopticon was gratifying to the young teacher, and helped fill the great need for adequate equipment to present lecture material to the students, but there remained gnawing at him the intense desire for more and better laboratory apparatus for his own experiments. Forced by circumstances to be largely self-taught, he struggled mightily to re-create the work of the great experimenters of whom he read in books; but he frequently found himself frustrated by the lack of suitable apparatus.

"When I read of the brilliant experiments of Tyndal or Liebig, I almost feel to despair of becoming anything like a successful experimenter," he wrote in the spring of 1882. The Academy budget was pitifully inadequate to provide what was needed, and improvisation led to frustration as often as it did to success. Efforts of the young teacher to "test the results of the electricity of the atmosphere" by means of the famous kite-flying experiment provided a serio-comic sequence that might have served as the scenario for a hilarious two-reeler farce when the motion pictures were invented some decades later. When the Academy did budget funds for scientific equipment—rarely more than $100 or $150 at a time—the difficulty of securing exactly what was wanted from the far-off supply houses in Philadelphia or New York was too often an added frustration.

In these circumstances, it was inevitable that the young man's thoughts should turn to the idea of pursuing his own education at one of the established institutions of higher learning in the East, even though the difficulties—chiefly financial —in the way of such a plan at first appeared insurmountable.

Once conceived, the idea took root and grew rapidly. First confided to his personal journal in mid-January as a "vague idea. . . . on which I have yet sought no counsel," the thought of a year at an institution specializing in scientific instruction was irresistible and its fascination grew steadily. By the end of March, the young man had sufficiently solidified his thinking to discuss the project with Dr. Maeser, who expressed hearty approval and went so far as to predict that the project would be given the young teacher as a mission call.

With this encouragement, James promptly sent letters of inquiry to Yale, Harvard, Cornell and Lehigh and later to some other institutions. While awaiting replies, he went to Salt Lake and obtained a personal interview with the President of the Church, John Taylor, who spent considerable time listening to the young man outline his proposed program, then gave his "decided advice" to go ahead with it.

James thereupon made a careful study of the prospectuses of the institutions to which he had written and decided, the advice of friends concurring with his own conclusions, that Lehigh University in South Bethlehem, Pennsylvania, offered a program best suited to his special needs and desires. A letter of application for entrance was sent to the president of that institution on May 19, 1882. On June 2 a favorable reply was received and the die was cast.

At the end of the BYA school year, James briefly debated whether to spend the few remaining weeks before departure learning or earning, and quickly settled on the former. His financial situation was so straitened that it could not be materially improved in a short time, and his earnest desire was to be as well as possible prepared to squeeze the utmost benefit from his time in the East. Accordingly, he laid out a schedule of home and laboratory study to "bone up" on his scientific courses, and especially to review mathematics and German, areas in which he found he might be weakest in relation to the entrance requirements at Lehigh.

After performing final services for BY Academy—including the outlining of courses of study in the various classes he had taught and the equipping and setting up of a new scientific laboratory better than any he had had access to while at the institution—he settled down to intensive study and other preparation for the big adventure ahead.

Finally, on August 26 he left Provo for Salt Lake City on the first leg of his journey.

# The Trip East

The bleak, monotonous stretches of Wyoming Territory's lonely prairies stared back through the grimy train windows all through the day of August 29, 1882, as young James E. Talmage looked out on them from the relative comfort of the jolting, sooty Union Pacific train that was carrying him to a new and exciting—and sometimes a little frightening—opportunity.

The landscape offered little of interest—nothing to compare with that passed yesterday in Weber Canyon, where Devil's Slide, Steamboat Cliff, Witches Rock, and other natural phenomena had provided a veritable museum showcase for a young geologist. The traveler spent most of the day, bundled in all available wraps against the penetrating cold that was encountered at the high altitude despite the date, in reading, and in looking back at the crowded, eventful days that had preceded the start of the journey. There were many memories, mostly pleasant; but the recollection of the long day and half night of helping to haul hay at Pa's farm, working against time to keep it from spoiling, still brought painful twinges to muscles which had grown unaccustomed to that kind of exercise.

One of the pleasanter memories was of the farewell party which the Sunday School and priesthood quorums of the ward had staged in his honor. He carried with him tangible mementos of the occasion: a Morocco leather writing case and inkstand, a travel set of toilet articles, a photograph album, and a gift of two dollars in cash from the boys of the deacons quorum by which he was deeply touched.

From time to time his mind turned solemnly to the deeply spiritual experience of receiving his endowments—at the Endowment House in Salt Lake City, by special authorization of President John Taylor, to spare him the necessity of the long trip to the St. George Temple—an experience to which his thoughts returned often, but of such holy nature that he refrained from confiding his impressions even to his private journal, noting that such a thing would be "far from lawful."

He had later been especially set apart, as for a mission, and been given a blessing. President Wilford Woodruff, counsellor to President Taylor, and Apostles Francis M. Lyman, Brigham Young Jr., and John H. Smith had laid their hands on the young man's head, Elder Young serving as voice. The young traveler felt deeply comforted in facing an unknown future in a part of the country strange to him, when he recalled that he had been assured that, if he remained faithful to his calling, he would find friends among strangers and success in his endeavors. He recalled, too, the admonition that he should attain his primary educational objectives and then return home, not tarrying to seek after degrees and academic honors; but that these things would come to him later if he followed the counsel which he had sought from the Lord's servants.

From time to time during the day he interrupted the course of his reading and his contemplation when occasions arose to converse with fellow-passengers, the talk always turning to "the Utah question," a lively issue across the nation in 1882. Discussions of the Mormon question continued through a good part of the night, for James and others who had stretched out on the seats were awakened around midnight to make room for additional travelers who were boarding the train at each stop, en route, as it developed, to an agricultural fair being held next day at Grand Island, Nebraska. The young Utahn gave up his seat to an elderly man and spent the remainder of the night standing in crowded discomfort, but engrossed in earnest conversation. Council Bluffs, end of the Union Pacific run, was finally reached after nearly 56 hours of steady travel from Ogden. A brief pause between trains and then back aboard the Chicago and North Western for the run on to Omaha and Chicago, which consumed another 20 hours.

A cold, stinging rain was falling in Chicago. Streets were muddy, skies leaden, and the whole outlook highly inhospitable to the eyes of a stranger, who confessed to feeling something "different from serene contentment." Problems of finding the agent of the Baltimore and Ohio Railroad to whom he had a letter by which he hoped to (and did) obtain a 20 per cent clergy reduction in the fare for the latter part of the trip, and in getting luggage transferred to a station in another part of the city, were worrisome but successfully met, and shortly after 5 P.M. he boarded the train for Philadelphia on the penultimate leg of the journey.

There was another cold and lonely stopover at 3:15 A.M. in a city which at that hour seemed to radiate anything but brotherly love.

Once more there was the problem of getting baggage transferred across town (different railway lines appear to have located their big-city terminals about as far from one another as possible in the early 1880's) and of keeping track of it until departure time. This one was solved by riding with the baggage transfer man, who drove furiously about the city for nearly four hours. Finally, at 8 A.M., the thoroughly weary traveler boarded the Pennsylvania and Reading for South Bethlehem, Pennsylvania. Two hours later he descended at that city, the cross-country trip behind him and the next and far more important phase of the big adventure immediately ahead.

# Lehigh

The first view of South Bethlehem, Pennsylvania, and of the "college grounds" of Lehigh University produced mixed emotions in travel-weary James E. Talmage. Natural elation at reaching journey's end and the thrill of anticipation were somewhat tempered by fatigue, loneliness and the feeling— common to travelers on the trains of the 1880's—of being "so dirty that I expected to be taken for a tramp."

A trip to a "barber and bath establishment" improved both the outward appearance and inward composure of the young man, who immediately set out to look for a suitable place to stay. The college boarding house was a logical first place of inquiry, but charges quoted on the spot were "far above those advertised" and some of the living arrangements appeared unsatisfactory to one who knew he must remain largely apart from many elements of the world in which he had come to live for a season.

A series of checks on a list of private homes which was provided him by college officials brought a deepening sense of discouragement. Families offered either room without board or board without room, and one senses in reading the journal account of the day's search the carefully concealed deeper reason for immediate rejection: the cost of daily living would be frighteningly high in comparison with the meagre resources at the young student's disposal. By mid-afternoon he confessed to "feeling the *blues* again, most decidedly." Just at this point a chance encounter with a man standing in front of his home developed at least a temporary solution. The man's wife had been considering the possibility of taking a boarder and a one-month trial was agreed upon to see if arrangements were satisfactory to both parties. The young stranger breathed a heart-felt sigh of thanks and felt a great load lifted from his depressed spirits. Later, due to problems within the family of his host, a Mr. H. W. Werner, James moved away and he made a number of other changes of residence during his stay in South Bethlehem; but this first stopping place was one that remained close to his heart. The warm hospitality of the Werners was never forgotten, and there was a more practical aspect to be appreciated, too. The price of $18 a month for combined room and board fit the young man's tightly restricted budget. The first night in his new quarters James settled his few belongings and made a detailed accounting of his finances, which he confided to his journal. It explains a great deal of his underlying uneasiness, his repeated moves (after leaving the warm haven of the Werners), his decision to use library and laboratory privileges in the middle of the day, so as to take advantage of those extraordinarily fine facilities while they should be available—and also to keep his mind fixed on things other than the pangs of hunger as he skipped lunch, obviously for economic reasons.

The "strict accounting" of finances showed that $61.10 had already been spent, for train fare (at reduced "clergy" rates) and the incidental expenses of traveling across the country. Having left Provo with $161 in ready cash, this left $99.90 cash-on-hand, while a $320 bank draft was deposited. This $420 (less ten cents—his accounting with himself was precise) was his total capital as he looked forward to a long and expensive year far from home, friends and further resources.

"God bless that little money to my good: for it has indeed been saved and economized to the very best of my ability," he wrote in his journal on September 4, 1882. " 'Tis Utah money and 'tis tithed, according to the rules of the Church, and 'tis honestly gained—*why may I not expect it to be blessed?*"

The young man's first encounter with student customs provides an insight into his philosophy as he settled into his new environment.

> Purchased a walking cane today for a few cents. This may
> seem a very trivial item, but it illustrates one of my favorite theories,
> viz, that a traveler should be strictly cosmopolitan, and ever con-
> form to the ways of the particular community wherein he may be.
> Nearly everyone carries a walking stick here, and my friend Mr.
> Werner informs me that I should do the same. So, I did it.

But he drew a careful distinction between this type of
conformity to custom and one which would be counter to his
beliefs.

> All the men smoke here; I do not intend to smoke for that
> reason, because by doing so I sacrifice a principle, but by simply
> using a cane I sacrifice no principle, but at the same time conform
> to [the customs of] the people here.

As time went on, he was to exhibit the same careful distinction in a variety of situations. He accepted with good
grace mild hazing imposed on all of the "fresh" (Freshmen)
at the college: the wearing of a distinctive small cap, the
seizure of his newly acquired walking cane by upper-classmen,
and other similar minor annoyances, but noted that "if any
very severe indignities, amounting to insults, should be heaped
on me, I should deem it my duty to retaliate." No such excesses were committed, however, and within a short time,
when the granting of upper-class laboratory and library privileges to the young man from Utah, on the basis of his performance in entrance examinations, convinced his fellow students that he was not a Freshman, he felt profound relief.
Outwardly he gave no sign, but his inward satisfaction clearly
showed in the exultant "aha!"—exclamation mark heavily
shaded—which he confided to the privacy of his journal. His
walking stick was returned and he carried it with quiet satisfaction as he observed the further manifestations of college
spirit, particularly the traditional clashes between Freshman
and Sophomore classes.

The Lehigh "walking cane" proved more than the "con-
forming of a traveler to the ways of a community wherein he
may be." The comfortable feel of the smooth wood and the
sense almost of companionship (if an inanimate object can be

a companion) appealed to the young man. The habit survived the transformation from youth to full maturity and became almost an identifying badge of a man who walked for both exercise and enjoyment whenever the occasion offered. In the last years of his life, after a bad fall in the mission field induced a near-crippling injury, James E. Talmage carried a very heavy walking cane as a matter of necessity. Until then, he carried a walking stick by choice much of the time when its use would not definitely be *out* of harmony with local customs, and it served as a pleasant reminder of that first encounter with college customs in 1882.

The young man got down to the serious business of academic work as quickly as possible, allowing very little to distract him from his basic objective in coming East to college, except for inquiries concerning Utah and "the Mormon question," which he was ever ready to discuss at any length. The formal call on the president of the university was promptly made and pleasantly completed. His credentials were found fully acceptable and he was referred to Dr. Chandler, the professor of chemistry, who was to be his special faculty advisor. A schedule was set up and the young student buckled down to work in earnest.

After carefully considering all of the possibilities, he enrolled as a special student. On the advice of Dr. Chandler, who checked his background and tested his knowledge and abilities, he scheduled Senior classes and was assigned a place in the Senior's laboratory (ending his Freshman status and attendant hazing). First term class schedule included chemical philosophy, metallurgy, crystallography, and a required course in physiology. Classes were over by 11:30 A.M. each day and "as I do not eat lunch" the young student could throw himself zestfully into laboratory work until the lab closed at 5 P.M.

The superbly-equipped laboratory was the apple of his eye, something of which he had long dreamed in the days when he had longingly read of such facilities and had spent long, weary, often frustrating hours constructing jerry-built substitutes from what materials might be available to conduct experiments and present demonstrations to his classes at Brigham Young Academy. He was keenly aware of the charge given him by the First Presidency before he left home, to avoid the pursuit of academic degrees and personal honors, but to acquire knowledge and bring it back to share with the people in Utah. "Like a bee out from the hive," he wrote in his journal, "may I add to the store of useful knowledge in our Mountain Home."

The laboratory and the library were facilities to which he could not have access elsewhere, and were to be prized accordingly. The library contained 30,000 volumes and "the leading periodicals of Europe and America": scarcely Harvardian by today's standards, but highly respected in 1882 and something of almost Arabian Nights-like wonder to a student from far-off frontier country where a collection of a few good books was a rare treasure.

James' skill in "phonography" once more proved a valuable asset. The lecture classes at Lehigh appear to have been precisely that, "the professors regarding themselves as lecturers, not teachers" who "talk on, caring little whether the students understand the subject or not, and to a slow notetaker, such is peculiarly disadvantageous." The taking of near-verbatim shorthand transcriptions required intense concentration and effort and the subsequent transcription was laborious, "but the two writings of the notes give me a better idea of the substance of the lectures than the hours other students spend struggling over broken up and disconnected sentences."

James' knowledge of phonography led to further activity of an unexpected nature. A "Workingman's Club" had been organized in South Bethlehem, and quarters provided largely through the efforts of Lehigh Seniors as a social service project. At the request of Dr. Coppée, senior professor at the University, young Talmage agreed to conduct a weekly class in phonography although he doubted that it would attract much interest or accomplish much in a practical way in the limited time afforded. The instructor was pleasantly surprised on both counts.

A group of fourteen appeared for the initial class period, and interest and attendance steadily grew, rather than waned, as the year progressed. When the final class session was conducted in August, 1883, just prior to the instructor's leaving South Bethlehem, members of the class presented him with an ebony, gold-headed cane, engraved with an expression of their appreciation. The event drew the attention of the Bethlehem *Daily Times,* which commented, "This is certainly proof that the gentleman bears with him in his departure from Bethlehem the hearty good will of his friends here."

Meanwhile, regular work at the university kept James fully occupied. Days began early and ended late. Weekdays were taken up by lectures and work in the laboratory. Saturdays were usually spent in the library, as were evening hours when time was available, or sometimes Saturday visits to the famous Bethlehem Iron Works and other major industrial plants where the theories of metallurgy, chemistry, electricity, and other sciences were taken from their familiar laboratory settings and put to work in full-scale earnest for the benefit of society.

Sundays were scrupulously kept free from work and generally devoted to going to church. There was no LDS branch in or near Bethlehem at that time and James visited a variety of denominations, sometimes two or three the same day. He was sometimes critical of elaborate ceremonies which he felt bordered on the pagan, but generally he sought out the good he could find in other churches' services, as he did in the chapel exercise at the University, which he chose to attend although he might have been excused had he so requested.

Extra-curricular campus activities were generally viewed from a distance, as it were, from the point of view of an observer and critic rather than that of an active participant. Founders' Day ceremonies on October 11 appeared impressive in the young Utahn's eyes (his twentieth birthday had passed a little more than two weeks previously) except for the

crowning social event, a dance—a "hop" in campus termi-
nology—in the evening. Watching from the sidelines, he found
the affair a startling contrast to the homespun dances he had
known at home.

"Artistic performance is here of course preponderating;
while its lack is all but universal at home," he noted. "But the
dresses, the unmistakably questionable ways of the dance are
surprising."

However, his role of spectator rather than participant
may have had other roots in addition to the feeling that dancing techniques at Eastern colleges were shocking. He carefully
listed his reasons for not taking an active part:

"1—One must know how to dance: I do not; 2—one must
wear a dress suit: I have none; 3—one must have a lady: I
have none; 4—one must hire carriage and pair for going and
coming, etc.: I cannot afford it."

There were some extra-curricular activities which drew
his active participation. He gave full support to clubs or
"societies" founded on academic rather than social interests.
The Chemistry and Natural History Society, membership
comprising Junior and Senior Class students in this area of
study, proferred him membership which he promptly accepted
and he was elected secretary of the organization at the first
meeting. He delivered technical papers before the Society at
suitable intervals and noted on at least one occasion that the
presentation was well received and that he "had the satisfaction (?) of a cheer" (question mark the diarist's own).

Class scheduling and examinations were found to be
somewhat informal and flexible, and in early October he was
astonished at being informed that the lecture portion of the
course in metallurgy had been completed and that students
might apply to take the final examination when they so
desired. James did so promptly, and found the exam to con-
sist of an hour's close questioning by the professor (no other
students being present), at the end of which the professor said
"quite satisfactory, Mr. Talmage," and the lecture course in
metallurgy was behind him.

Some other examinations came at irregular intervals, but most of them were near the end of the scheduled term, which ended with the Christmas holidays. His term report brought the happy news that he had failed in no subjects and stood No. 1 or No. 2 in the class in a number. The final examination in chemical philosophy must have been particularly rigorous, for James was concerned that his mark was "really low," although concern was somewhat alleviated by the fact that it was "first on the list," leading the class.

Tensions and natural anxieties of "exam week," when most of the term examinations were given, extracted their toll from a young man who rarely took things lightly and was usually more tightly wound inside than he allowed to appear on the surface. A week before Christmas, he confessed to feeling signs of illness and depression and that "I really believe that if I had time to be ill, I should be so, very."

The Christmas holidays brought respite and were passed for the most part very quietly. James attended many church services and spent a good deal of time in the library and in visiting industrial plants.

The beginning of the second academic term on January 11, 1883, with a new schedule of classes brought a fresh reminder of personal financial problems. The bill for last term's laboratory breakage and special equipment was $55.39, startlingly high in comparison with the registrar's pre-term estimate that it might run $60 for the full school year, and the $35 advance deposit which had been made. The incident brought on a fresh rash of efforts to reduce basic living expenses, which were already cut to the bone.

As was to be expected, the second term passed more routinely than the first, when all things had been new and strange. Journal entries were fewer and shorter, reflecting the rapid passage of time devoted to intense work on weekdays and nights—on one occasion he notes having cultivated the friendship of the janitor at the library and having been able to work there until 2:30 A.M. From time to time budgetary problems forced themselves to the forefront of his attention and there would follow another change in eating habits or living quarters, never fully satisfactory.

The final academic term slipped by even more rapidly in much the same pattern except for the addition of a considerable number of field trips, on which the classes observed geologic phenomena or major industrial works in the area. These were always of special interest to the young man from Utah. Second term and year-end exams were passed successfully, including one in German, a subject he had not pursued in any class course at Lehigh but which he undertook at the suggestion of his faculty advisors. The exam, given informally at the home of the professor of languages, proved not too difficult on the basis of what James had learned from Dr. Maeser at BYA. James had his first surprising encounter with the "honor system" when he applied for his final examination in botany and was given a set of questions and told by the professor to take the examination in his own quarters. He did so, with scrupulous regard for the rules.

As the college year approached its close, he gave increasing attention to the possibility of remaining another year in the East, to be spent at another institution where he might find instruction in a number of branches of science in which Lehigh did not specialize and which would be valuable additions to the store of knowledge he hoped to take back home. The financial problem was severe, of course, but he had managed to get through the year at Lehigh, and a letter from J. M. Tanner at BYA in Provo assured him that the necessary money could be raised and added to his present loan. Professor Tanner also sent a draft for $50 on the same terms, to relieve current financial pressures.

The accounting which James recorded in his journal at the close of the formal college term indicates the closeness of the reckoning he had been required to maintain over the months. Total expenses since leaving home, including those of traveling, came to $457.15, to which had to be added $19.50 for "books for college ordered from home." Subtracted from the original stake of $500, this left him with "about $30 of

my own money," a slim enough margin to explain his under-
lying financial worries and frequent changes of living quarters and eating habits over the months past. It explains, too,
why the recently received $50 loan from Professor Tanner
provided a feeling of comfort and security out of proportion
to its actual size, and why $15 received from an industrial
firm for a chemical analysis he had performed for them
(passed to him by Professor Chandler) was virtual manna
from heaven.

By this time he had just about made the decision to spend
another year in the East, even though financing the prolonged
stay would depend "absolutely on what I could borrow."
Looking back over the academic year just completed, he
expressed thanks to the Lord for the protection and peace
which had been afforded him and set down his conviction
that "the information gained here in any single week would
repay me for the expense and trouble in coming here."

"My successes, by the help of God, have been greater than
I had dreamed," he wrote. "Now may He grant me sincerity
and humility in the use of them."

The certificate he received from the secretary of the
faculty attested full university credit for the following courses
of study, pursued on campus or passed by special examination:

Freshman classes: German, botany, elementary chemistry.

Sophomore: Qualitative [chemical] analysis, physics, German, chemical preparations, assaying, blowpipe analysis.

Junior: Chemical philosophy, toxicology, quantitative
analysis, anatomy and physiology, crystallography, organic
chemistry, iron metallurgy, minerology.

Senior: General metallurgy, quantitative analysis, chemistry applied to arts, medical chemistry, agricultural chemistry,
historic, dynamic, and economic geology.

He was urged to stay and complete the requirements for
a formal degree; but, mindful of the admonition he had
received from Church authorities before leaving home "not
to seek after personal honors or degrees," he was not to be

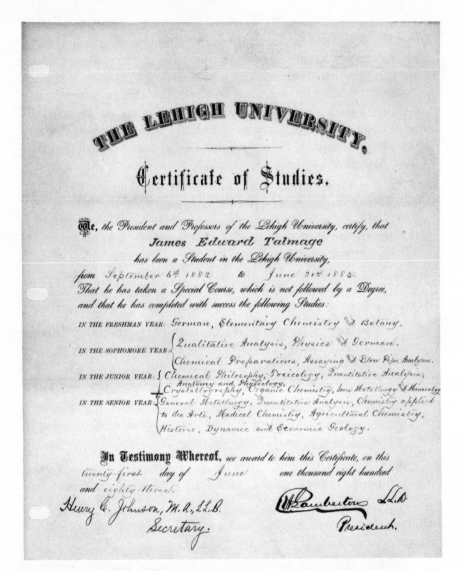

The certificate presented by Lehigh University to 20-year-old James E. Talmage at the conclusion of the academic year 1882-83. Although James had spent only one year at Lehigh, credit was awarded for work in Freshman, Sophomore, Junior and Senior classes.

swayed from his decision that if he were to remain in the East, it would be at another institution where he could pursue lines of study not featured at Lehigh. The Lehigh faculty voted to award him the institution's degree when he completed the formal requirements "whether here or elsewhere."

Graduation requirements which were lacking were mainly in the field of mathematics, and James, all regular classwork behind him for the year, immediately began "boning up" in this field. His reaction to this work disclosed a peculiar mental attitude which he held at this time and perhaps never completely lost and which was probably due, at least in part, to the environment from which he had come and which so strongly emphasized the need for practical applications of scientific knowledge. He wrote:

> For some reason, I have always been inclined to shirk all mathematical studies which do not admit of direct application. It is a humiliating confession to make, yet my mind is so trained as to *abhor* all but the concrete. Yesterday and today I have been trying to "get down" to higher algebra and analytical geometry. I can understand the subjects easily when I fix my mind upon them, but it is absolute torture for me to pursue the study for an hour. I never dreamed of becoming so callous mentally in this respect.

If this reaction to mathematics was somewhat surprising, James' reaction to *it* was typical of his intellectual approach: "If for no other reason than this, now I shall pursue my mathematical training in earnest."

Vacation time offered considerable relief from the tightly restrictive schedule which had held him for the past nine months. He considered working during the summer months and obtained a number of job offers, but when he balanced the remuneration against the added costs of commuting, etc., which they would entail, he perceived that the net return would be almost negligible. He decided his time would be more profitably invested in making full use of the University Library and in field trips to study industrial operations, museums and other attractions in the area.

The decision to remain in the East having been made, the question was the choice of institution, and the decision quickly boiled down to consideration of two institutions, Yale University at New Haven, Connecticut, and Johns Hopkins in Baltimore, Maryland. After much soul-searching and seeking of counsel, including correspondence with both institutions which indicated he would have no problems of accreditation at either, he chose Johns Hopkins. For the particular courses of study he was seeking, the Baltimore institution ranked with any in the nation, and the prospective over-all cost appeared to be considerably lower there than at Yale.

Word came from Brother Tanner at BYA that administration and faculty at the Provo institution would almost certainly approve an expanded loan to finance another year's study, and when a personal advance of $100 from Utah backers (Bro. Tanner himself, $50, W. H. Dusenberry, $30, and W. N. Dusenberry, $20) reached him, James considered that the die was cast. He formally applied for admission to Johns Hopkins and shortly afterward received word that he had been accepted.

On September 5, 1883, he left South Bethlehem—destination, Baltimore.

# Johns Hopkins

James' arrival in Baltimore in September, 1883, was in many ways a replica of his coming to South Bethlehem a year previously. At the same time there were significant differences, which clearly reflect the passage of that twelvemonth time and some subtle changes it had wrought.

It was once again the coming of a stranger to a strange place, the beginning of a new adventure, with no one knew what experiences in store. However, this time it was not a young man on his first solo venture so far from home. Rather it was a seasoned traveler, who could anticipate many of the routine situations and problems and take them in stride.

Arrival time was late evening, after a stopover in Philadelphia and a missed train threw him several hours behind schedule. Unruffled, he spent the night in a modest hotel and on the morrow lost no time in locating the University buildings and seeking a boarding house in the vicinity. By mid-afternoon he was installed "in a small, third story room at the residence of a Mrs. McCarty, No. 223 Saratoga Street." It proved a pleasant and congenial place to live, although he was to change quarters a number of times before the year was out, in the same pattern and for the same economy-based reasons as the previous year in South Bethlehem.

Once settled in his living quarters, James lost no time in making himself acquainted with his new environment. In many ways, the move from South Bethlehem to Baltimore was a bigger change than the move from Provo to the Pennsylvania community. That had been a challenging experience, a move from the still-frontier West to the industrialized East, from the friendly warmth of home to the midst of strangers with strange customs. Yet South Bethlehem proved to be a small community, exuding the close-knit atmosphere of small communities everywhere. Baltimore was something else entirely, and the "transplanting from a little country town to the heart of a great city" was a major change, immediately felt but which long continued to provide new (to the observer) contrasts and additional food for thought.

He had come to look upon South Bethlehem almost as a second home, where he had so widely found friends among strangers, as he had been promised that he would in the patriarchal blessing given him before he left Utah. In fact, he wondered within himself if he "dared" to become so closely attached to a "strange place" and sternly reminded himself that he had come as a missionary with a definite mission to accomplish, "viz, to gain knowledge by experience and experiment, and when the time shall come to return home in safety, there to resume my labors and apply the beneficial acquirements made here." On this point he wrote further:

> The facilities for study in the East are such as to readily allure me to stop here, were I to give way to feelings when making a comparison with the means of study at home. However, I must be no more attracted than is the bee which visits gay flowers in its quest for honey; its end is to return to the hive with its treasure, else it would die. *So will I* unless I fulfill my mission properly.

James was frequently troubled by inner doubts as to whether he had made the correct decision in coming to Baltimore for an additional year's study. That the decision to spend a year at Lehigh had been the right one, there could be no doubt. His own carefully considered reflections had been reinforced by counsel taken with Brother Maeser, with ward and stake leaders, and, finally, with the First Presidency of the Church. But the decision to stay on at Johns Hopkins had, by force of necessity, been his own.

"I have been prayerfully reflecting for two months, but I have been able to gain no direct counsel from any at home,"

James E. Talmage, as he looked shortly after attaining his majority. This was just prior to the beginning of classes in 1883 at Johns Hopkins University.

he wrote in his journal. "I feel, however, that I am where the Lord would have me."

Settling into his new quarters in Baltimore and putting aside his moments of self-doubt, James quickly took advantage of the array of new and unusual opportunities for learning which were offered him. He found not one but two research libraries which overshadowed even the one that had so impressed him at Lehigh. In addition to the university's own, there was that of the Peabody Institute, and he spent much time in both in the days between his arrival and the beginning of formal classwork on September 25. He also visited an impressive array of public utilities and industrial establishments and took advantage of the offerings of museums and botanical gardens.

When the academic year began on September 25, regular work in class, and especially in the laboratory, became of paramount importance. The course of study still focused on chemistry, but major emphasis was now on the organic rather than the inorganic branches of that science which had formed the nucleus of the course at Lehigh. Biology assumed a major role in the course of study. Although James did not pursue a medical course as such, the medical aspects of chemistry were emphasized in his selection of study course, and he frequently attended medical lecture classes, when time permitted, for which he was not formally enrolled. His early home atmosphere when his father had been the village doctor left a lasting impression and deep-seated interest in medicine and he had given serious consideration to making it a career.

As James became better acquainted with his fellow students and mingled with them to a degree in after-class discussions and activities, he underwent an experience which shocked him to his very foundations. From the moment of leaving home he had been acutely conscious of the different standards of conduct and morality in the "outside world," but until he mingled with the students at Johns Hopkins he had never encountered anything quite like this.

Fellow students at Lehigh had presented a strong contrast with young people at home, but the more sophisticated and worldly men at Johns Hopkins openly boasted of their romantic conquests and outright immoralities. These were not just a few ruffians, looked down on with disgust by the better element comprising the majority of the student body, but a substantial number of those he met on campus. They were young men of refinement, in terms of conventional social graces. They came from highly respected family backgrounds. They were "well behaved" in conventional situations, were pleasant company, and could converse intelligently on science, art, economics, current events—all of the subjects which refined and intelligent people discussed.

The deep sense of shock experienced by the young man from Utah was the same that countless young people from Latter-day Saint communities have experienced—and continue to experience and doubtless always will—when they first directly encounter worldly attitudes toward sexual morality that are completely foreign to the principles they have been taught.

In time, James came to accept the situation as he found it and his fellow students as they were, although it never ceased to trouble him greatly and to occupy a large portion of his leisure-time thoughts. They, in turn, learned to accept the young Mormon for what *he* was, including his recurrent outbursts of protest and admonition when their group discussions returned to certain subjects.

One incident in particular stood out in James' memory and he many times related it in later years. One student, who appeared to pride himself on his very excesses in debauchery, sometimes deliberately baited the Utahn to provoke him into argument, asserting that the latter was missing many of life's pleasures, without valid reason and without reasonable prospect of compensating reward. On one occasion, in the presence of a sizeable group of students, the young Mormon picked up the challenge:

"All right, William," he said, "let us for the sake of argument suppose for the moment that your belief is correct and there is no God and no hereafter. Suppose, also, we were both to die tonight. Which one of us would have lived the fuller life?"

"Oh, I suppose people would say you had," William conceded, with an airy wave of the hand. "But I prefer to take my reward in tangible enjoyment as I go through life— you can have the empty satisfaction of a more flowery tribute in your funeral oration."

"I grant you that I should have little more to show for my way of life," said James. "But now let us for the sake of further argument assume that *I* am right in my belief in a living God before whom all men must appear for an accounting after they have passed from this mortal existence. Again we suppose that we are both to die tonight. *Now,* which of us would have the advantage?"

For a moment William appeared to weigh this question with the same lofty detachment he had accorded the previous one. Suddenly, however, the meaning of the stipulation he had lightly accepted fully penetrated his consciousness. The theoretical situation took on a terrible reality.

In a flash, the young man's whole appearance changed dramatically. Color drained from his face, which took on an unhealthy hue of yellowy wax. His eyes seemed to sink into his head and reflected stark terror.

"My God!" he burst out, in tortured agony of spirit, "may it not be so!"

The mood quickly changed, the discussion ended, and the attention of the group shifted to other matters. But William never again baited the young Mormon, although there was no sign that he had changed his way of life.

James, for his part, could never forget the look of sheer terror that had transformed William's face, and especially the tragic irony of his having called on Deity to deny His own very existence.

Much of James' time in Baltimore was spent in observing and analyzing the social structure and institutions of the Maryland metropolis. Some of this was in connection with university courses, in organized groups, some of it personal observation in the course of daily living. He saw and was appalled by the teeming misery of the masses living in abject poverty in the slums, especially in the bitter cold of winter. He was especially disturbed by the plight of the very old and the very young, the former generally neglected and abandoned to an appalling fate, the latter fashioned by their environment for a lifetime of almost hopeless resignation to conditions of subhuman standard.

The relative informality of his course of study as a special student offered James wide opportunity to broaden his education from the narrower limits of the classroom and laboratory, but his chief interest and activity continued in the chemistry laboratory. Dr. Ira Remsen, a distinguished chemist and scholar, was head of the department at Johns Hopkins and early in the year offered the young Utahn a station in the special Fellows' Laboratory where he could work directly under Dr. Remsen's personal supervision. The offer was gratefully accepted, and the close association with the department head left a lifelong imprint on the student.

James' term of study at Johns Hopkins was threatened to be cut short by a disaster in far-off Provo early in 1884. On January 30 he read in the Baltimore newspapers that Brigham Young Academy had been destroyed by fire. Details were meagre, but by the newspaper account it was clear that the destruction had been virtually complete, although there had been no loss of life. In the journal, James wrote:

> This may change all my plans—and may cause my very early return home—for I can scarcely hope for financial aid from the institution in such a crisis. I wrote to Brother Maeser tonight and asked him for full particulars and instructions. If the institution is to pass through a trying time, it is my duty to hold myself ready for any call.

A "hastily written" letter from Brother Tanner two days later brought more detail and on February 13 a communication from Brother Maeser informed James that the Academy would definitely carry on and that the apparent calamity might prove to be a blessing in disguise "for so much the sooner will a suitable building be at the disposal of the institution." The letter also informed him that while he could of course expect no further advance on salary from the institution, he should stay to complete his year of study if he could possibly borrow the money from other sources. Later, through Brother Tanner, a bank loan was arranged which added interest charges to his already considerable financial burden but did allow him to follow his planned program at Johns Hopkins to its conclusion.

The academic year ended early in June and James passed such examinations as he was scheduled to take (some of his courses being on special student basis not entailing exams) and concluded his affiliation at Johns Hopkins. He noted that it had been "highly satisfactory to my mind" and that "the experience of the year has been much broader than that of the preceding one at Lehigh, though the Lehigh year formed the foundation of the year just closed."

Finding that he could travel home more cheaply by going to New York and joining a company of returning missionaries due to leave the metropolis in a few days' time, James spent the interval in taking final advantage of the library and museum facilities in Baltimore and visiting historic sites in the area. On June 18 he boarded a boat for New York, for the first stage of the journey home. During a stopover in Philadelphia and in New York he went to the offices of leading suppliers of scientific and laboratory apparatus to establish contacts for future dealings when he would be back at BYA.

On the evening of June 20 he boarded the Chicago, Lake Erie and Western Railway for the long journey to Utah. The trip required almost five full days, but passed without incident and quite pleasantly. Arriving in Salt Lake City on June 25, James paused only to report briefly to the General Authorities of the Church, then proceeded on to Provo.

First days at home passed in getting reacquainted with family and friends, horseback (and how good it felt to ride a fine horse!) visits to his grandmother in Pleasant Grove and to other near and dear ones outside of Provo. Tales of the wonders of the big eastern city had to be told and retold for younger brothers and sisters who had grown astonishingly in two years. More formal talks were given at Church meetings on Sunday and during the week when MIA groups assembled.

But very soon James was back in harness at BYA, assisting Professor Maeser to prepare the following year's "circular" in the early days of July.

At the July meeting of the Board of Trustees, the executive committee fixed James' salary for the coming year at $1,000, "with an increase if the (institution's) net profits exceed a certain sum."

James sincerely hoped it would be a profitable year, for he faced a personal debt in excess of his basic annual stipend. An exact accounting discloses that total expenditures for the two years study in the East (including travel) were $1089.60. Personal loans which were largely responsible for his being able to stay for the second year included those from J. M. Tanner, W. N. Dusenberry, W. H. Dusenberry, George Q. Coray, J. B. Keeler and A. Singleton.

"I am under heavy obligation to those named, for in most instances the loans were given unasked," he wrote. "My second year's course depended absolutely on the kindness of my friends. May I ever remember it!"

# CHAPTER EIGHT

# Back Home

In a very short time the initial excitement of homecoming wore off, and James found himself so rapidly moving back into the old routines that, in some ways, he might almost feel he had never been away. At the faculty meeting of Brigham Young Academy next following his return, he was put back in his old post as secretary of the faculty, with all the attendant routine duties. He was almost immediately returned to his position as a home missionary, and was assigned to speak in the various wards on Sundays, many of them at considerable distances from Provo. He re-assumed the old practice of delivering lectures to MIA and other groups— including on one occasion a Methodist youth organization— on request. Before the end of the year, more than thirty such addresses were recorded, many of them entailing considerable travel. At the first quarterly stake conference following his return, young James E. Talmage was named alternate to the High Council and on September 29 was ordained a High Priest by Stake President David John.

There were also many differences brought about by the two years of study in the East. There was an inward assurance felt by the young man himself, and there was a new added respect for himself and for his qualifications, as shown by others. No longer did he feel an aura of vague resentment from even a few fellow faculty-members because of his youth. When Dr. Maeser found it necessary to be away from the Academy for a few days, James E. Talmage was named acting principal, and after a time he was officially appointed first counsellor to Dr. Maeser in the presidency of the Academy.

Recognition of his newly-acquired academic standing came also from sources outside Brigham Young Academy. A delegation from the People's Party came to urge him to be the party's candidate for the office of territorial superintendent of schools in the fall elections immediately following his return. He expressed appreciation for the honor but had to decline, not only because of his obligation to the Academy, but also for the very practical reason that he was ineligible to hold public office, not being a U.S. citizen. This obstacle was removed at the first opportunity. When the District Court convened for its fall session on September 15, 1884, the first time it had been in session and reasonably accessible since he attained his legal majority, James E. Talmage applied for citizenship, passed the required tests, and received his naturalization papers as a citizen of the United States less than a week before his twenty-second birthday.

James noted with considerable satisfaction that he was now a registered voter in the precinct, for, while his interest in politics as such was virtually nil and he tended to avoid active involvement unless it was thrust upon him, the right of the franchise was an especially precious thing. These were the days of the bitter struggles for control of the Territorial institutions between the People's Party and the Liberal Party.

The former party was the political organization of the LDS people—open to those of all religions and joined by some non-Mormons, but essentially composed of those who believed in the aims and ideals of liberty which had motivated Brigham Young's original pioneer band as they came West and settled in the Valley of the Great Salt Lake. The Liberal Party was the party of the "outsiders," whose core was the Washington appointees who were generally hostile to the Church and everything connected with it, and who were regarded by Church members and sympathizers in the same light in which the post-Civil War "carpetbaggers" were viewed in the South.

Feelings between the two groups grew increasingly bitter and it was a rarity to find contact between them on any basis except that of open hostility.

On the evening of July 4, 1885, James reached Salt Lake City en route home from a trip to Idaho and tells of finding "a feeling of considerable excitement" due to a People's-Liberal clash during the day. He recounts:

> We learned on inquiry that the United States' flag had been raised on several buildings at half mast, our people not feeling to rejoice on this the birthday of Independence, but rather to mourn for the death of Liberty in our midst. I feel sincerely to say "Amen" to the sentiment so expressed. We have true cause to regard Liberty as dead or dying in Utah; the oppressions and persecutions of late are exceedingly severe. The self-professed *loyal* citizens of the city chose to regard this act as an insult to the flag, and they tried with their usual feeling of vindictiveness to incite a riot.

On July 4, 1887, the People's Party in Provo invited the Liberals to forget their differences briefly and join in a community observance of Independence Day. The Liberals refused.

One year later, however, James found himself involved in a similar situation more or less in reverse, and experienced curiously mixed feelings. A joint People's-Liberals Independence Day observance, "all creeds and parties," was carried out in Salt Lake City, at the instigation of the Liberals. Somewhat surprisingly, the youthful James E. Talmage (still more than two months short of his twenty-fourth birthday) was asked by Church authorities to come up from Provo and represent the People's Party on the speakers' platform. He accepted, and found himself riding to and from Liberty Park, site of the public celebration, in an elegant carriage set aside for the day's orators with companions definitely not of his own choosing. There were Judge H. H. Benson "of anti-Mormon fame"; Judge C. C. Goodwin, "the present editor of the Tribune—the foulest of foul sheets"; and Judge Zane, "the present Chief Justice of Utah, the 'Mission Judge' as he is called [because] he is so unmeaningfully severe on all of our people who come before him."

James privately expressed his strong distaste for "mingling with the oppressors and persecutors of our people in raising the cry of Liberty and Freedom," but conceded that acceptance of the proposal for a joint observance was proper and that Church members should "agree with them [the Liberals] in all things that are just and fair."

The Independence Day observance itself appears to have been a great success. Governor Caleb West presided, flags waved, bands played, and the designated orators spoke on patriotic themes. James occupied the rostrum for some fifteen minutes to discuss "The Characteristics of a Free Man."

The return to the city was an experience in itself. The official carriages, one carrying the Governor and the day's Marshall, the other transporting the speakers, were formally escorted by a platoon of cavalry. The youngest member of the speaker group noted, tongue-in-cheek:

> And herein we were furnished with a striking example of the true meaning of honor and dignity. To be guarded by an escort of horsemen is certainly an honor; but to be almost suffocated by the dust as a result of the galloping and maneuvering of the guards is of a different nature. For my own part, I would have gladly dispensed with a degree or two of honor to have secured a trifle more comfort. However, it was a grand affair.

Though it was possible to meet with the Liberals on terms of civility for special brief occasions, basic emotional feeling was deep rooted and in quite another vein. James mourned on another occasion:

> Persecution has grown almost to a mania among our enemies and would-be destroyers. It seems literally impossible that a "Mormon" can ever obtain justice in the courts. . . . The fulfillment of prophecies of old is so marked that the wise remark, "When the fig tree puts forth her buds, ye know that the summer is nigh" has a deeper and wider meaning than before.

Back at BYA, James' position continued to advance. His salary was increased modestly from time to time, but his gratification was somewhat tempered by the fact that actual payment might be held up for long periods. In August, 1886, for example, he noted that $800 of his previous year's salary—

two-thirds of the annual total—was still unpaid, occasioning severe personal embarrassment as his own obligations must in turn remain unsatisfied.

"I have always tried to avoid debts, but sometimes fail," he noted laconically. With the greater part of his previous year's salary unpaid, the failure is easy to understand.

By this time, however, James was viewing his own and the Academy's financial problems in a different perspective. On March 1, 1886, he was notified by the "heirs and assigns of the late President Brigham Young" that he had been appointed a member of the Board of Trustees of the Academy. Three of the original seven-man board appointed by Brigham Young himself had died and Don Carlos Young, James E. Talmage, and John Q. Cannon, in that order of seniority, were named to fill the vacancies.

The new board members found the financial condition of the Academy to be even more strained than they had previously known or imagined. At times there was serious question whether the institution would have to suspend operations, at least temporarily, but ways and (usually strained and contrived) means were somehow found to carry on.

Fund-raising activities for BYA took James into many scattered communities, as did his weekly assignments as a home missionary. Field trips to examine (with increased understanding and interest since his training in the East) the geology of the region, carried him into remote areas. The field trips were sometimes made alone or with one or two companions, but frequently with one of his classes from the Academy. He recognized the problems and heavy responsibilities of escorting groups of young people over considerable distances and into sometimes hazardous conditions, but he also remembered his own feelings, as a student, of the immense value of such practical outside-the-classroom study and his promise to himself that, if he should become a teacher, he would make such trips a feature of his instruction.

Whether alone or in a group, James' travels were a constant reminder to him of the relative primitiveness of the Territory and the strong contrast with travel in the East.

The railroad had come to Utah in 1869, and branch lines to the north and to the south connected with the transcontinental trunk line, but the branches extended for relatively short distances and travel beyond the reaches of the railroad was of pioneer ruggedness.

On one occasion, after filling a home missionary assignment in Salem, James was driven by horse and buggy to Spanish Fork but arrived too late to catch the train. There being no alternative if he were to meet his Monday morning classes at the Academy, he walked back to Provo, leaving Spanish Fork about midnight.

On another occasion, after a field-study trip to the Tintic District mines, the party was travelling late Saturday night in order to avoid the necessity of so doing on the Sabbath, and a drenching cold rainstorm suddenly broke, turning the dirt roads into quagmires and coating everything with icy sleet as temperatures plummeted. Those in wagons sheltered themselves as best they could with tarpaulins and bedding, but James was on horseback, exposed to the full fury of the storm. Despite the extreme discomfort of cold and wet, he found himself so fatigued that he fell asleep several times in the saddle. Cavalrymen in the Civil War reported many similarly curious experiences, some actually dozing off while their mounts were jumping fences or stone walls.

On a trip to Idaho to study the peculiar chemistry of the waters at Soda Springs, James relates that on leaving the railroad at Montpelier he and a companion were driven to Paris by a former student, Thomas Jones, who volunteered his services even though the undertaking was "somewhat dangerous on account of excessive high water in the Bear River." This appears to have been a definite understatement.

"For a distance of about six miles, the road lay entirely under water, so deep in places as to overflow the top of the wagon," James noted in his journal. "We had to perch on the seats like fowls on a roost."

In May, 1887, James undertook his first extensive trip primarily in the interest of geological study, through central

The group of young geologist-explorers which hiked to the floor of the Grand Canyon of the Colorado, along the historic trail of Major Powell's 1869 expedition, in the summer of 1887.

and southern Utah and into northern Arizona. Travel was by horseback, with three pack animals in addition to the individual mounts, to serve a party of seven. Others in the party were Samuel Allen, Joseph Nelson, and Willard Croxall, students of Professor Talmage at BYA, and M. W. Pratt, Thomas Wilson, and B. E. Driggs, friends of the other three.

Major objective of the expedition was to visit, and actually descend, the Grand Canyon of the Colorado. To reach that wonder of nature, the party had to traverse two-thirds of the length of the state, obtaining en route an impressive view of the variety of Utah terrain. Rugged canyons, hot, dry deserts, wind-eroded cliffs, and the cool beauty of evergreen forests produced their varied impressions.

As the party neared the Grand Canyon, they were warned by ranchers living in the area of the dangers of attempting a descent into the gorge, dangers stemming not only from the precipitous nature of the terrain but also from the scarcity of potable water along the way. Having come this far, however, the travelers were not to be turned from their objective.

The party found and followed the historic trail taken by Major Powell and his party in 1869, although at times "to keep on the trail was a difficult task, as landslides and washes, fallen trees, and brush have obliterated it in many places." At the foot of the extremely steep and hazardous stretch known as Jacob's Ladder, they found the skeleton of the mule killed by the Powell party, an event recorded in the official report of that historic trip.

At nightfall on the second day of the descent (June 16), the Talmage party reached the bottom of the canyon and threw themselves down on the sandy banks of the Colorado, "a deep and rushing stream, the rocky sides of the canyon rising on either side to a height of 3,000-5,000 feet, an awefull sight. . . . with darkness adding a feeling of terror to that of awe."

The return trip, over the same trail they had descended but which now provided them an exhausting climb, "severely taxed our endurance [although] much suffering would have been averted if water were procurable." The party finally reached the rim after covering fifty rugged miles in less than three days, nearly exhausted but happy with their adventurous exploration.

Professor Talmage's dreams that night "were of rippling streams and clear lakes. I was drinking and bathing," he recorded.

As the group started north on the return journey, Professor Talmage's fine Morgan horse was found to be so worn that he traded it for a desert pony, a rugged animal suited to the country but "wild and unbroken." There were some violent bucking episodes when it was questionable "which suffered more, horse or rider," but the pony eventually accepted his new role and performed adequately thereafter.

The traveling party disbanded in Manti, where a financial settlement was effected and it was found that the cost of the expedition had been $50—not per person, but for the party of five. The $10 apiece expense included instances of renting overnight pasture for the animals at what was described in at least one instance as "an exorbitant rate."

When he made the trip to the Grand Canyon, James thought it was to be a farewell to Western country for a season, prior to another period of study in the East. He had thought about such a project for some time and had gone so far as to consult with BYA authorities and finally with President John Taylor, and had obtained approval for his planned venture all along the line.

The death of President Taylor put a temporary halt to James' plans and before they could be put back into operation, problems developed at the Academy which led to a request from Stake President A. O. Smoot that James cancel his plans for further Eastern study, or at least postpone them until conditions should improve. James agreed to do as he was requested, although he was somewhat astonished by his own acquiescence, which was "in direct contradiction to the state of my personal feelings."

Having made the decision, James settled down to academic and Church duties with his customary energy, and he also undertook greater involvement in civic affairs than ever before. He was among the active supporters of the establishment of the "Provo Free Reading Rooms" (forerunner of the Public Library), delivering public lectures to raise funds for the project, and early in 1888 ventured into the political arena for the one and only time in his life.

On February 6, 1888, at the nominating convention of the People's Party, James E. Talmage was selected as Councilor from the Third Ward and "accepted only on the counsel of the authorities, for I truly dislike political office." The reason for the urging of Church officials was that the issue of preserving or repealing the ordinance prohibiting the sale of liquor within city limits was under hot debate and the People's Party wanted an able public speaker and dedicated champion for their cause.

James was elected and he zealously fought for an anti-saloon ordinance in Provo, but it was a losing battle from the outset. However, the young Councilman commanded the respect of his peers, including those of the majority with whom he so frequently clashed on questions of policy. In June, 1888, when the position of Third Ward Alderman became vacant through resignation, Councilman Talmage was urged to seek the position not only by the anti-saloon contingent but also by those whom he had most vigorously and consistently opposed on the Council. His uncompromising integrity had impressed political friend and foe alike, and his acceptance of the new position, which included the duties of magistrate for the area represented, resolved an impasse which had developed on the Board of Aldermen. Although already overburdened with work, James accepted the draft, resigned his position as Councilman, and assumed the new and time-consuming responsibilities.

Before it started, James' relatively brief experience of "holding public office" had almost been blocked by a serious accident, one of several critical accidents or illnesses which threatened to bring disabling injury or untimely death to James E. Talmage over the course of his lifetime. On February 20, between the date of his election to the City Council and that of actually taking office, he was pouring molten slag from an assay crucible into a mould in the laboratory when some material inside the molten mass exploded, scattering the remainder and hurling some of it directly into the professor's left eye.

The pain was frightful and it at first appeared that the eye had been permanently destroyed, for the molten matter had actually penetrated the eyeball. Weeks of intense physical suffering were compounded by no one knows what mental tortures as he must inevitably have been thinking of the tragic loss of sight of his brother Albert, who had lost one eye and had the sight of the other destroyed by "sympathetic" reaction. But expert medical attention, frequent administration by the priesthood, and the motherly nursing of Sister Josiah Cluff into whose home James was induced to move temporarily after a grim attempt to care for himself in his bachelor's quarters, eventually brought full recovery with no permanent impairment to his vision.

James took the oath of office as Councilman on the very evening of the accident, with his eyes tightly bandaged. For a time thereafter, all but the most pressing of appointments and duties were cancelled, but by early March he was seeing clearly and carrying out his full schedule of duties.

The combination of academic and civic responsibilities provided one of the busiest and most pressureful periods of James E. Talmage's always-full life through the remainder of 1888. Although he had no inkling at the time, both his BYA and Provo Alderman's experiences were rapidly approaching their end. However, the heavy press of official duties of all kinds was temporarily pushed into the background by an event which changed the course of his personal life for all time and gave it lasting and ever-increasing enrichment. This was his marriage to Merry May Booth, a native of Alpine, Utah County, and a former student at BYA.

# Merry May-Maia

On the first day of the year 1888, twenty-five-year-old
James E. Talmage was in a sentimental mood that, most
unusually for him, was allowed to appear openly in the entry
in his journal. Personal loneliness and hunger for affection
show clearly in a brief outburst that is normal for a young
man of 25, but most untypical of the tone of the entries in
the private journal James had now kept for a dozen years.

He confessed, with a trace of bitterness, that in earlier
years he had scoffed at the idea of conventional love between
men and women and had "boasted in my mind that I could
do without it," presumably in order to devote his time, thought
and energy to study and work.

James then discloses something that had not been even
hinted at in previous journal entries: that prior to his departure for study in the East he had for a time changed his earlier
attitude and had seriously contemplated marriage. When the
decision to go away to college was definitely made, he called
on his reserves of self-discipline to put other things aside, his
budding romance among them, and it had never come to
flower. There is no hint of the identity of the object of James'
earlier affections.

Following the New Year's Day outpouring of his heart,
James gave no further indication of this trend in his thoughts
in his journal entries for the next month, but there is other
evidence that it had not passed from his mind, or even been
relegated to a minor role.

Friends of James E. Talmage in later years told of hearing him relate stories of his deep preoccupation with seeking

a wife and his worry that his austere way of life to this point had not well fitted him for this task. He made it a matter of prayer, as he did all things of serious import in his life, and, according to the stories told by friends, finally placed the matter before the Lord in terms almost of a business proposition:

"Lord, Thou knowest that I have very few acquaintances among the young women of Zion, and Thou hast full knowledge of them all. Guide me to her who is meant to be my help-meet in life."

This paraphrase, from the recollection of friends who heard James tell the story in later years, may or may not be strictly accurate, but there is no doubt that some such thought filled James' mind and entered into his prayers at this time. There also appears to be clear evidence that his prayer was richly answered.

Early in February, James went to Salt Lake City on Academy business. From there he proceeded to Kaysville near the eastern shore of the Great Salt Lake "for the purpose of making examinations and collecting specimens; and according to previous appointment with some friends." This project was duly carried through, and James spent the daylight hours of February 4 in the company of Golden Kimball, a former student, in collecting scientific specimens and making observations at the lake shore.

A heavy black line is drawn across the journal page at the conclusion of this routine account of the day's activities, but the entry below the line is separated from what went before by much more than this arbitrary barrier. A different tone, a different feeling, pervades the two following pages, as the outpourings of a young heart bursting with happiness struggle mightily to find escape and expression through the too-narrow outlet of a pen trained and long disciplined to deal only with cold fact and objective observation.

In the evening James had "called at the residence of a former student at the Academy, the present teacher of the District School in this town, and above all a very dear friend."

> It was not without previous thought [though entirely without previous written intimation] that I arranged to stop in Kaysville, for I had intended and desired to make the call alluded to. This intention and desire I believe influenced me more strongly than the "specimens" and "examinations of the lake shore" to make the present trip, for these pursuits could have been postponed to other and more favorable times. But I wished to see my friend—*Miss May Booth*—a noble woman devoid of the blemish of artificiality so widely affecting our girls; a sincere woman, and above all a woman who makes the living of her religion the supreme object of her existence. . . . Though our associations have never been other than those of teacher and student, I had (very recently) made the matter of my interest toward her a subject of sincere prayer, and I felt that God approved my decision. This evening I asked . . . if she would be my wife. Her positive answer was given exactly in the way in which I had asked of the Lord as a sign of his approval. . . . My love toward her is no idle fascination—it is a love founded on respect and esteem, and as such I feel it will live.

The way it did live, and never cease to grow and expand and find new bonds of common interest and more and deeper reasons for existence and of mutual expression, formed a magnificent story over the next forty-five years.

On this day of early February, 1888, the happy, newly-engaged couple decided that a specific date for the wedding would have "to depend upon circumstance, but should not be long delayed."

Almost incredibly, the following day, despite the exuberance which must have filled his heart to bursting, James E. Talmage, diarist, returned completely to his earlier cold reserve and objective treatment of factual matters. Two days later came the "draft" of the young educator for the Provo City Council election, noted earlier. Two weeks later he met with the terrible accident with exploding slag which almost cost him his sight. These things, and the routine of Priesthood and Academy duties, occupied nearly all of his journal entries, though not, we may be certain, all of his thoughts. Only when there was specific reason to refer to the planned wedding does it gain even passing mention.

"Miss May Booth" was the tenth and youngest child of Richard Thornton and Elsie Edge Booth, who had embraced the Gospel in their native England and crossed the plains by oxcart in coming to Utah. One son, Ebenezer, fifth child of the family, had been born on the way in the best of pioneer traditions. The Booths had settled in Alpine, Utah County.

The tenth child of the family was born September 29, 1868 and christened Merry May Booth. At least this is the name that was written on the Alpine Ward record sheet the day the baby was given a name, although there always remained some question as to whether the spelling "Merry" was fully intended or was at least partly an accident.

Some of the Booth children had been learning a Sunday School song about "the Merry, Merry Month of May," and when the decision as to what to name the baby had not been reached and the hour for Fast Meeting was coming close, one of the children was heard singing the song and the suggestion was made that the baby be given the delightful name "Merry May." The suggestion was accorded immediate and unanimous approval, although no one appears to have raised the question of spelling. Some family members felt that it was intended to be the conventional "Mary," but retaining the same joyous, ringing sound as the words of the song. Whatever the parental intent, one of the children ran ahead to the chapel to inform the bishop how the certificate of name and blessing should be made out, and it was officially written "Merry May Booth" and so allowed to stand.

As she grew older, the young lady herself resolved the question by using only her middle name, except when legal or other requirement made use of the full name a necessity. Within a few years of their marriage, James had his own special name for his life partner: *Maia*, name of the Roman goddess of Spring, which became the most frequently used form of address he employed save when more formal usage might be required in public.

By any name or mode of spelling, May Booth Talmage was a remarkable woman and a perfect helpmeet to her husband. A woman of striking beauty, as pictures taken in younger years clearly show, she was never vain. Her faith in

The Booth family in November, 1891. Sitting, left to right, John E., Mother Elsie Edge, and Robert E. Standing, left to right, Hannah, Jennie, Alfred Lewis, Merry May, Wilford, and Margaret. As can be seen, May's picture was inserted some time after the group picture was taken. When the group picture was taken, May was awaiting the birth of her second son, Paul.

the Gospel was deep and she was truly dedicated to its principles and always ready to do willingly whatever *she* might be
called upon to do—rather than to envy another's calling and
consider her own assignment harsh.  Generous to a fault, she
found joy in giving to others, whether her own by ties of blood
or marriage, or to total strangers.  She lived through many
periods of hard times—"recessions," "depressions," or "financial panics," when desperate job-seekers ("tramps," they
were called then) went from door to door seeking odd jobs
in return for a meal to keep them going.  No one was ever
known to be turned from her door hungry, and some holidays
such as Thanksgiving or Christmas it was not unusual to have
a half-dozen such "tramps" warmed and fed during the course
of the family dinner and evening.

She was scrupulously honest, sometimes to the point of
naiveté.  She could not countenance even the most remote
appearance of dishonest dealing on her own part, and by this
very reason may sometimes have been made the victim of
sharp practices by others—something she freely admitted, but
preferred to the alternative of compromising her own standards to the slightest degree.

Intelligent, educated, cultured, she shared her husband's
interests and played her own prominent role on Church aux-
iliary boards and those of women's organizations.  She was at
home with rich and poor, with the great and the humble—
but never with the thrill-seekers, the self-seekers, the vulgarly
coarse, or the hypocrites.  She visited the great cities of her
own country and of Europe, but she never lost her deep love
for Alpine, its people, and its honest values.

As years went by, James E. and Merry May—Maia—
became more and more as one, growing ever closer with the
passage of years, even though the press of his official duties
kept them physically miles or thousands of miles apart for long
periods of time.  James did learn to express his personal feelings as eloquently as he expounded on the Gospel, and his
letters on anniversaries and other special occasions (when so
often he had to be far away) were prized by Maia far above
material gifts.

In the end, May outlived James by some eleven years. They were years devoted to children and to grandchildren, to Church duties and to good works. But for *her* they were essentially years of patient waiting. When her own hour came, very early on the morning of April 6, 1944, there was no doubt that this was the time of joyful reunion to which she had been looking forward over all of those years.

In the spring of 1888, when James was 25 years old and May was 19, the future was an exciting and challenging road which stretched out ahead, with no one knew what turnings. The date for the wedding was first set for May 30, but was postponed due to the sudden and unexpected death on May 27 of the father of the bride-to-be. The date was reset for June 14, and was made a quiet and simple observance due to the recent family bereavement. The young couple traveled to Manti where the Temple had been dedicated less than three weeks previously (the Salt Lake Temple would not be completed for another five years) and on the appointed day were married by President Daniel H. Wells.

The event was noted in a brief article in the June 15 edition of the *Utah Enquirer,* published in Provo, and the *Deseret News* carried the following under the heading, "A Benedict Now."

> We have received a card on which is the following statement: "James E. Talmage and Merry May Booth, married at Manti, June 14th, 1888." There it is in a nutshell, in the Professor's terse and sensible style. Plenty of prosperity to the estimable couple.

On their return to Provo, because of the recent bereavement, the couple declined a reception proposed to honor them, but quickly set about establishing their first modest home.

Many of the attendant duties were strange and foreign to previous habits and training of the young science teacher. A five-room cottage was rented, quite near the Cluff home where James had been living. Shopping for furniture and household items, and their installation and arrangement, were part of the basic homemaking in which James took deep pride, but the details of accomplishment provoked some wry comments. On June 26 he noted:

> Busier than ever, preparing for household responsibilities. Tacking down carpets, putting up stoves, etc., etc. Pleasant occupation? Yes, I suppose so; it is said that wise men always like the inevitable. . . . I try to believe that I am wise in such matters, but I must confess that sometimes I feel very foolish. But I am happy and proud and above all thankful to my God that such duties now rest upon me.

The sense of satisfaction and thankfulness increased immeasurably when the period of spade-work ended and the new home, consisting of bedroom, combined kitchen-dining room, living room, and a "cozy little front room called by my wife 'the parlor' and by myself 'the office and study room,' " was finally in order, something to be enjoyed rather than the instigator of a seemingly endless series of work details. The period of peaceful enjoyment, however, was to be short-lived.

During the very days when the Talmages' little home was being furnished and arranged, some far-reaching changes were being effected in the Church educational program. A Church Board of Education was established and Dr. Maeser was called to serve as general supervisor of Church schools under its direction. Plans were announced to establish a number of stake academies; and James E. Talmage was asked if he would serve in the Salt Lake City institution. He promptly replied that he considered himself subject to the call and direction of the authorities of the Church, and that he would respond at once to whatever call he might officially receive. He noted:

> Our [BYA] Board of Trustees do not view this movement with full favor, thinking that the interests of the Academy will in some degree suffer, it being relegated to the position of a stake academy —one among many—while the central institution is to be established in Salt Lake City. The Trustees urge my remaining at the [BY] Academy at least during the ensuing school year, and offer me the position of Principal. The President of the Board directed me to prepare the Circular for the next academic year.

James immediately went about the duties assigned to him, but declined to commit himself on his response if he should receive an official call to another assignment.

The call was not long in coming. Within a week, Dr. Maeser was advised by the General Authorities not to resign as principal of BYA, and Professor Talmage was informed by President Wilford Woodruff (president of the Quorum of the Twelve at this time, the First Presidency not yet having been reorganized since the death of President John Taylor the previous July) of the desire of the Apostles to call him to Salt Lake City very soon.

"Nothing yet can be definitely decided upon," Professor Talmage noted on receipt of this message. "The circumstances under which the Church Authorities are at present placed [the threat of imprisonment under the retroactive application of the odious Edmunds-Tucker Act] are such that they cannot be easily reached."

Meanwhile, on July 3, James was approached by a member of the Board of Regents of the University of Deseret with regard to his joining the faculty of that institution. This was the second time he had received an informal approach from that quarter. He replied, as he had on the first occasion and as he had to the proposal of the BYA Board, that he considered himself subject to the call of the General Authorities and that he would make no commitment that might conflict with such call.

On July 16 the specific call came, a letter from President Woodruff stating officially that it was the desire of the authorities that Professor Talmage should move to Salt Lake City as soon as possible and labor in the school interests there.

James travelled to Salt Lake that same evening and, by appointment, was met by President Angus M. Cannon of Salt Lake Stake, who conducted him "along circuitous routes" and finally into a room "in which I was surprised and overjoyed to meet several of the Apostles—President Woodruff, Apostles George Q. Cannon and Joseph F. Smith, and several others who had long been in exile and hiding."

After a warm exchange of greetings, the assembled authorities outlined to the young professor the plans for the Salt Lake Stake Academy and asked him to assume the position of principal of the institution. This was confirmed in writing over the signature of President Woodruff and was, of course, accepted by the professor. He began his new duties immediately, commuting from Provo at first. A subsequent meeting of the Salt Lake Stake Board of Education, which Professor Talmage attended by request, fixed his starting salary at $1700 a year after the professor had declined to suggest an acceptable figure.

"The brethren seemed very anxious to allow more; but I am fully satisfied with the figure under all circumstances," James noted. Evidently his period of service on the BY Academy Board had taught him a great deal about the fiscal problems of new and growing educational institutions.

The remaining days of July, 1888, were perhaps the busiest that James' very busy life had known to this time. Duties of Alderman (entailing the conduct of regular justice court sessions) and packing for departure at the Provo end, and seeking a suitable place to live at the Salt Lake location, added to the already heavy pressures of winding up duties at BY Academy and preparing to open a new institution in Salt Lake City. It was no wonder that the harassed professor observed that "such strong medicine as moving away should be taken in moderate doses."

Eventually, however, the necessary things were accomplished. A three-room cottage at 32 Centre Street—on the westerly flank of what has since become known as Capitol Hill and overlooking the great Tabernacle and the partly-constructed Temple—was secured as a prospective new home and the final arduous packing of all the things housed in the old home (including some thousands of pounds of mineral specimens) was at last completed. Final session of Justice Court was conducted and Alderman Talmage's resignation duly submitted and accepted, including the approval of a claim of $38.80 for services rendered.

The *Utah Enquirer* editorialized: "The resignation of Alderman Talmage will be universally regretted. He was one of the few members of the present city council in whom the people have placed implicit trust. Besides, he was as efficient as trustworthy."

Early on the morning of August 2, 1888, Professor and Mrs. Talmage took the train to Salt Lake, this time going not as visitors but as permanent residents. The rest of the day was even more hectic than the final days of preparing to leave Provo. Getting their possessions moved from the railroad depot to the new living quarters, finding places to put them in the three small rooms, getting "at" the items needed immediately, filled a completely exhausting day. By nightfall, however, there was at least sufficient order to find chairs to sit in, a table from which to eat, and a bed to sleep in.

A new home was founded and a new chapter of life had been opened.

CHAPTER
TEN

# Beginnings of LDS College

Getting settled in a new home is an exhausting task. Assuming a new job is a major adjustment. When the two things have to be done at the same time, and especially when the job entails virtually the establishment of a new institution, the combined assignment is bound to tax the energies and abilities of even the most disciplined administrator. Young Professor Talmage threw himself into the oversize task with all his might, ever conscious of the critical time pressure under which he was laboring.

Basic aims of the institution were set forth in the official letter from President Woodruff, providing insight into the long-range plans for the Church educational system, as they were then conceived. The President wrote:

> It is the general feeling that we should have a first-class institution here [in Salt Lake City] under Church auspices, where sooner or later every branch of learning can be taught and acquired —an institution that will successfully vie with other denominational academies and colleges that are now in existence and that may hereafter be established in our midst.

President Woodruff went on to convey the request of the Church Board of Education that Professor Talmage take the position of principal of the new institution. It was not a "call" as for a mission, but an offer "if it is agreeable to you and the terms can be made mutually satisfactory."

However, President Woodruff added:

> Should you agree to take charge of this institution, we trust that you will enter upon it in the spirit of a missionary as well as

that of a teacher, and while it is proper that you should receive suitable compensation, we sincerely hope that this will not be the ruling feeling with you, or with anyone who may engage in a similar capacity, but that it will be with you a labor of love as well as one of remuneration.

The offer was accepted in this spirit and, as already noted, the new principal not only declined a later request by the Board that he suggest a salary figure but actually proposed a slight reduction in the figure first advanced by the Board.

The timetable called for the academy to open its doors under the new program not a year or more hence, but that same fall of 1888, a scant six weeks after the first meeting of the new principal with the Board on July 17. These were days when the pioneer spirit still prevailed and hardy men and women were accustomed to taking time by the forelock and acting quickly and decisively. Nevertheless, six weeks was a short span into which to cram the writing and publishing of a "circular" (catalog), the preparation of suitable quarters, assembling a teaching faculty, securing needed materials and supplies, planning and scheduling courses and classes, the examination of candidates for admission, and the myriad other tasks attendant to the undertaking. The time pressure was made no lighter by the fact that Professor Talmage was, on the date of the initial meeting with the Salt Lake Stake Board of Education, still a member of the BYA faculty and not only a resident but an Alderman of Provo. The move to Salt Lake City with its many time-consuming details had to be fitted into those same few weeks.

Somehow the many-faceted undertaking was accomplished and on September 3 the new Academy opened its doors in the old Social Hall. The first-day attendance was "a most flattering 215, with several more applications under consideration." The enrollment was large enough to tax the facilities of the little Social Hall, which was not designed to accommodate a multi-class schedule.

Problems of textbook selection, familiar to educators of every generation, were complicated in the Salt Lake City of

1888 by severe limitations on available supply. The city was no longer the pioneer outpost it had been prior to completion of the railroad in 1869, but there were still many items in very limited supply, school books among them.

The situation was met with the simple, direct action which is the essence of pioneering: use what is available, adapt whenever possible, and yourself construct what is still lacking.

To the new principal's already overcrowded schedule was added the assignment to write an elementary textbook on "Science" suited to the needs of a generation untutored in this area of learning and to many of whom the very word was a distasteful denial of the profound faith on which their way of life was founded. Professor Talmage's assignment to write a primer in the field of science was subsequently followed by the First Presidency's request for another and somewhat more advanced text.

The results were the *First Book of Nature* which went to the printer in mid-November, 1888, and *Domestic Science,* which came off the press in January, 1891. The former is a little volume of 265 three-by-five-inch pages, written in near-record time under heavy pressure and which the author noted was "an obligation undertaken purely as a mission." The latter was a considerably more substantial volume of 331 larger pages, written over a longer period of time on the basis of planning to meet the need for "books written in the spirit of the school system of our people" and which were in the specific area chosen by the Church Board of Education as that of most pressing need. On publication it carried a brief foreword signed by all three members of the First Presidency and a shorter message from Dr. Maeser as General Superintendent of Church Schools. The Presidency noted that a committee of Church educators "heartily endorsed it" and expressed pleasure in recommending it "as well adapted for use in our Church schools, also in the Mutual Improvement Associations, and for general reading." Dr. Maeser "earnestly recommended it to all Church schools for adoption."

The new Salt Lake Stake Academy managed to operate successfully and, within the physical limitations of space, materials and funds, continued to grow. On May 15, 1889, the name of the institution was officially changed to "Latter-day Saints College," the name under which it operated until the closing of its purely academic branches in 1931 and which is still used by the Business College, only currently-surviving branch of the original institution. (For a time, many years later, the institution adopted the more pretentious title of "Latter-day Saints University." This came to be recognized as unjustified, and the earlier "College" designation restored in the late 1920's.)

The press of official duties at the College was augmented, as always, by the growing pressure of outside duties, which tended to pile up, as they had at Provo, until the schedule became too crowded and some things had to be curtailed or dropped. But for every item eliminated, two more seemed to arise to take its place and the pressures never appreciably lessened.

James E. Talmage's fame as a lecturer on both scientific and religious subjects had preceded him to his new home and he was besieged with requests to speak before various Church, civic, and social groups throughout the area. He had an innate dislike of refusing such requests and there is no doubt that he honestly enjoyed the role of lecturer. Consequently, he tried to fill as many as possible of these assignments although the strain grew steadily heavier. At first, the school board strongly approved these outside appearances as they served to publicize the infant academy, but the demands for lectures rapidly increased to the point where President Cannon authorized Professor Talmage to turn down—in the name of the Academy Board—any which imposed too heavy a strain.

On one occasion, when he went to Bountiful to meet a request to speak on one of his most popular subjects, "Stimulants and Narcotics," James learned something of the difference between the public image generated by his lectures and teaching and his physical appearance. He had arrived at the meetinghouse a little early and was chatting with acquaintances when an elderly stranger approached.

"I heard you addressed as 'Brother Talmage,' " said the old man. "Has your father arrived yet to deliver the lecture? I should like to make his acquaintance."

Told that this was the lecturer in person and the principal of the new Salt Lake Stake Academy, the questioner burst out with a startled:

"Why, bless me! You're only a boy!"

Boyish-appearing or not, young Professor Talmage continued to have his fully adult duties added upon. In April, 1889, on the day following the close of General Conference, the newly-sustained First Presidency called a meeting of Church school administrators and teachers. A major item of business was the appointment of an Examining Board for all Church schools, consisting of Dr. Karl G. Maeser, Professor J. M. Tanner of BYA, and Professor Talmage. The new board was charged with the responsibility of passing on all prospective teachers in the Church school system. In the future, no teacher would be engaged by any Church school until he had obtained a certificate from the board.

Shortly afterward, in early May, the General Board of Education for the Church conferred new and special honors on the three members of the examining board. Each was given the title "Doctor of Didactics," with an added designation indicating the specific field of achievement of the holder: Professor Maeser became "Doctor of Letters and Didactics" (D.L.D.), Professor Talmage "Doctor of Science and Didactics" (D.S.D.), and Professor Tanner "Doctor of Mathematics and Didactics" (D.M.D.). Each was presented with an elaborate certificate attesting the new honor, signed by President Wilford Woodruff and George Reynolds, secretary, on behalf of the Church Board of Education.

The *Deseret News* of May 8, 1889,[1] reported the conferring of the new titles and diplomas, congratulating the recipients and noting that "it is the desire of the [Church] General Board

---

[1]A clipping of the *Deseret News* announcement and comment carries the date "Wednesday, May 8, 1888," but this is obviously a typographical error. The proper date is clearly 1889. May 8 fell on a Tuesday in 1888, on a Wednesday in 1889.

[of Education] that the titles associated with the degrees be recognized and used in the schools and among the people."

The new honor was deeply appreciated by the recipients, but James could not but be aware that the title would not be accepted in the academic and scientific communities beyond the confines of the Church educational system. However— although James could not know this at the time—it would not be long until honors and titles of the kind accorded full recognition would be added.

While the new doctoral degrees did not in themselves add to the workload of the three recipients, their positions as members of the examining board imposed increasingly time-consuming responsibilities.

The demands were heavy but the satisfactions of service and achievement were great. The new college continued to grow and prosper and the new Church educational program was taking hold. Members of the Church Examining Board noted with considerable satisfaction that the "new education" was steadily becoming better understood and accepted, and when, in May, 1891, LDS College presented the first graduate degree under the new program, Dr. Talmage felt double satisfaction as a member of the board and as principal of the college. His personal pleasure was still further increased by the fact that the recipient of the degree was Willard Done, his own assistant at LDS College since its inception.

While the growth and development of the young academy and the "new education" occupied the center of Professor Talmage's professional attention in these years of early development, many important events were occurring in his personal life.

"Vine Cottage," the three-room first Salt Lake City home at 32 Centre Street into which the newlywed Talmages had moved in August, 1888, was found increasingly inconvenient on closer acquaintance. In February, 1889, the couple moved into slightly larger rented quarters at 86 Centre Street, in the Nineteenth Ward. They still had only three rooms, but larger rooms and more conveniently arranged on the ground-floor

level, as contrasted to the two upstairs rooms at the old location. In addition there was a cellar, a "summer kitchen"
(screened-in back porch), and a stable. Best of all, there was
a water pipe which came right to the door—difficulties and
inconvenience of obtaining pure water had been a major problem at No. 32. The total of these attractions was sufficient
to overcome Professor Talmage's intense distaste for the task
of moving, but there was yet another benefit to be claimed:
rent at the new and larger quarters was less than at the old,
$11 a month as compared to the $14 the Talmages had been
paying.

The young couple was not to remain long in the new
quarters, despite all their attractions. Just a year later, in
February, 1890, an opportunity came, and was quickly
grasped, to purchase a lot on which to build a home of their
own.

The idea of building and owning a home had been a
high-priority objective since the Talmages had been first
married, and especially since they had moved to Salt Lake.
It had had to be delayed for financial reasons, analysis of
which has a strangely familiar sound to ears of those living
three-quarters of a century later. Professor Talmage noted
with concern:

> Property in Salt Lake City has been raised to fabulous prices.
> The place is said to be undergoing a boom, and in many cases the
> cost of land is fifty times greater than it was a few years ago. In
> but few places in town can lots be obtained at less than $1,000 a
> rod-foot, the usual depth being ten rods.

When Soren Iverson, father of LDS College student
Heber C. Iverson, expressed a desire to have the Talmages
as neighbors and offered a two-by-ten-rod tract of his land
for $1,300, the opportunity to buy substantially below the
going market was quickly accepted. The location, 330 East
Seventh South, in the Second Ward, was a little far from the
center of the city in those days but "a pleasant and healthful
neighborhood." One of the great and lasting attractions proved
to be the Iverson family, who were the best of neighbors in

times of sickness or of health and who became staunch, life-long friends.

Having purchased the land, Dr. Talmage lost no time in proceeding with the construction of a house. On March 3 a contract was drawn with James W. Eardley, calling for the construction of "a small, cozy home—six rooms, with accessory closets, pantry, etc.," to be finished early in May if the weather were favorable. The weather declined to cooperate and there were the inevitable problems in obtaining building materials, and it was noted on May 27 that "the day named in the contract for completion of the construction is now three weeks gone, and the house is far from being finished."

The rental agreement for the premises at 86 Centre Street was finished, however, and on May 28 the family moved in the new home, "camping out" in makeshift fashion while the work of completing the house was carried through. Unplanned delays were not all on the side of the builder, however. When Dr. Talmage contracted for the building of the new home, he expected to pay for it with money which he had loaned to a businessman friend "repayable on demand." When the demand was made, the borrower found his funds were temporarily tied up in real estate deals and it was not until February, 1891, that the loan was repaid and Professor Talmage was able to pass on to Brother Eardley, the builder, final payment for the house. The builder had been understanding of the situation and had never pressed for payment, but Dr. Talmage's own great relief when he could fully discharge the debt clearly shows through. He wrote in sincere and reverent gratitude on February 9, 1891:

> At present, I am out of debt for my home. Thank God for this! True, my house is not finished and furnished in all particulars, but it is a goodly home, and the Lord has given it. Of late I have been greatly reduced for lack of means; indeed, I have had to solicit loans to pay my fare on lecturing tours. Yet, I feel rich— wife, son and home, and a name in the Church of God. May the Lord in mercy keep from me all that is inordinate in the craving for worldly wealth. There is much in this world that is better than money.

When the Talmages moved into the new home, it was not as merely a couple, but truly as a family. On May 21, 1889, a son had been born, the first of eight children with whom James and Merry May were eventually to be blessed, seven of them growing to maturity. The joy of parenthood, the thankfulness to the Lord for this gift of a living being filled the hearts of both parents to overflowing. As days, months, and years went by, the joy and the thankfulness grew and flourished, as did the child, who was given the name of Sterling Booth Talmage.

In the summer of 1890 an epidemic of typhoid raged through Utah, and first James and later May were stricken so severely that at times both their lives were despaired of. Eventually, however, both fully recovered and neither suffered any permanent ill effect. One notable "plus" came from the trying experience: the acquisition of a family doctor who also remained a cherished lifetime friend, the then-recently-graduated Dr. Charles F. Wilcox.

During the period of his own convalescence, in the late summer of 1890, Professor Talmage made frequent reference to his work with the microscope, giving demonstrations for the entertainment of the family at the farm, putting his considerable collection of slides in order and making new ones. For a long time the microscope had been more than a laboratory tool for the student and teacher and was about as close to a genuine hobby as anything James E. Talmage ever embraced. He found real enjoyment in its use and maintained his interest throughout his life. Home evenings with the microscope became a feature of the Talmage family life as the children grew up and all of them down to and including the youngest, and their friends, were thrilled by the disclosures of the world of wonders that are hidden to the naked eye but which blossom forth in such incredible color and marvelous detail under the penetrating gaze of the microscope.

The microscope was also to play a very important role in shaping the course of Dr. Talmage's life.

By 1890, he had established correspondence with other devotees of the microscope in other parts of the nation and abroad, exchanging scientific slides and information. But it came as a complete surprise to James when on March 5, 1891, he received a letter from the secretary of the Royal Microscopical Society of London, notifying him that he had been elected a Fellow of that distinguished body.

To accept the proferred honor would entail more than the acquisition of an aura of prestige and the right to append the letters (F.R.M.S.) to one's name. A Fellow of the Royal Microscopical Society would not only be expected to maintain an active correspondence and exchange of slides and specimens with other Fellows around the world and to receive and entertain such of them who might pass through Utah—normal "routine" tasks that would not be onerous—but also to attend at least some of the annual meetings of the Society in London.

"I hardly felt that my circumstances and financial standing warranted my assuming so much," Dr. Talmage confided. He took counsel, not only with his own heart and mind and earnest prayers, but also with the First Presidency of the Church. The Church authorities counselled Dr. Talmage to accept the proferred honor without delay.

"This counsel I shall follow, trusting that all will be well," he wrote. A solution to the immediate financial problem did present itself very soon, in an unlooked-for way.

In late 1890 the Salt Lake Literary and Scientific Association had appointed a committee to study the plight of the Deseret Museum, which had suffered greatly from the lack of skilled direction since the retirement of its curator, the venerable Professor J. L. Barfoot, some time previously. Dr. Talmage was a member of the special committee and he vividly remembered his first contact with the Museum when he was a very young man, and the kind assistance he had received from Professor Barfoot. James had then and there acquired an ambition someday to find a post, even the most humble, with the Museum and contribute to its welfare. In 1890-91, in spite of the heavy press of duties already upon him, Professor Talmage volunteered to assume the duties of curator of the Deseret Museum, without any definite arrangements for remuneration.

For years Dr. Talmage had built and maintained his own collection of scientific specimens. After taking the responsibility for reorganizing and maintaining the much larger Museum collection, he soon decided that he could not successfully build two collections simultaneously; he transferred his private collection to the Museum and integrated the two.

There may have been some expectation of future recompense, but Professor Talmage had asked for none. It came as a complete and gratifying surprise when the Board of Directors of the Literary and Scientific Society, in April 1891, voted to pay him $2,500 for his collection, plus $500 for his volunteer services to date as curator. The way was open to finance a carefully budgeted trip to Europe while providing for wife and child at home. In view of Dr. Talmage's status as a full-time employe of the Church educational system and of the fact that he was urged by the Church authorities to attend the meeting of the Microscopical Society in London for the purpose of making the Latter-day Saint people known for good and establishing a line of communication between the Utah culture and the world scientific community, the First Presidency appropriated $350 toward the financing of the journey, the remainder of the expense to be borne by Dr. Talmage personally. The meeting of the Society was scheduled for June 17 in London, which required Dr. Talmage to leave Salt Lake City a few days before the end of the academic year.

The brief period from the late summer of 1888 to the spring of 1891, so eventful in the family life of the Talmages and in that of the infant LDS College, had also been one of immense significance in the history of the Church and the Latter-day Saint people. No attempt will be made here to examine and analyze those turbulent years in detail—this being the field of historians, who have devoted a great deal of attention to this era and doubtless will devote a great deal more in the future—but a brief glimpse of the historic backdrop may be appropriate to this consideration of the life of a man who was deeply stirred and affected by it.

This was the time of the very bitter struggle for control of the Utah Territory between the Latter-day Saints who had founded it and the Federally-appointed officials whose chief aim in life often appeared to be the persecution of the saints and the destruction of their institutions.

A typical confrontation between the two opposing groups came in the Salt Lake City municipal elections early in 1890. On election day, February 10, James recorded a summary of his own observations and thoughts concerning the campaign as follows:

> The Liberal Party have boasted of their intentions to steal the city; and in their confident hopes have failed even to try to cover up their infamy. Whatever charges the People's Party prefer against them they straightway admit and boast of their perfidy. Thus, in consequence of the irresponsibility of the Liberals and their open efforts to enrich themselves at public expense, the People's Party have spoken of them as "carpet-baggers"—and at once the Liberals adopted the carpet bag as their emblem and have even set it above the country's flag.
>
> The People's Party proved that hundreds of men had been brought from the railway camps, mines, from Ogden, Denver, and even as far away as Iowa to vote here today. Such arrivals have gone about the streets with badges upon their breasts declaring their home. Our enemies have learned that peace is a principle of our faith and not fearing [armed] retaliation they have been bold to make any assault.
>
> One of the pre-arranged tricks of the election was to get their [the Liberals'] votes early polled, then to obstruct the other voters in the exercise of their rights of franchise. The People felt it their duty to strive for all their rights and the call was made for voters to be early at the polls. I went before 5 A.M. and found a hundred already there. When the polls opened, fully 300 men were in line. Many were in position at 12 the previous night and remained there until voting began at 7:45 A.M.

Next day, February 11, the not unexpected but nonetheless deeply galling results were known and drew this comment from James E. Talmage:

> The result of the election is known and—the Liberals have succeeded in stealing their way into power. This city, the central city of the Saints, the seat of the First Presidency of the Church is now in the hands of the enemy. The Lord's will be done. He doubtless has His reasons for what is. Perhaps this will teach us

humility, and liberality. As a people, we are not entirely free from bigotry or intolerance. If we are made better by the experience, then all is indeed well with us.

On the national as well as on the local scene the persecution of the Latter-day Saints and, in particular, their practice of polygamy, continued to swell. On June 10, 1890, the decision of the Supreme Court of the United States in the long-pending case concerning the Church was published, several days after it had been handed down. The decision approved as constitutional the confiscation of Church property. The saints were stunned. Their enemies, of course, were jubilant and lost no opportunity to rub salt into the wounds of the Mormons.

Some three months later on Sunday, October 6, at the morning session of the Semi-Annual General Conference, the historic Manifesto was delivered by President Woodruff declaring to the world that the practice of plural marriage was no longer taught or sanctioned by The Church of Jesus Christ of Latter-day Saints and formally stating that the Church would henceforth abide by the law of the land in this matter in accordance with the principle set forth in the Church's twelfth Article of Faith.

James E. Talmage was present in the Tabernacle when the Manifesto was delivered, and was deeply impressed. In his journal he placed clippings from the *Deseret News* containing the account of the Conference session, including the full text of the Manifesto itself and that of the thirteen Articles of Faith which had been, by unanimous vote, re-adopted and sustained by the congregation just prior to the presentation of the Manifesto.

"This manifesto has caused much comment among the Saints," James wrote. "Some regard this step as one of retrocession, others look wise and say, 'I told you so.' Since this document was issued I have prayed for light as to its true import; and I see in it nothing but good for the people."

The publishing of the Woodruff Manifesto did not abruptly end the persecution of the Latter-day Saints or the bitter feelings between them and the more fanatical of their persecutors. It did, however, mark a definite turning point in the history of the Church and its relations with the world. In the private writings of James E. Talmage, this fact is apparent, not so much in any direct statement or observation as in the decreasing reference to and concern with the political struggles in Utah.

More formal notice of the change in relations between the Latter-day Saints and their "Gentile" fellow-citizens of the United States came in the spring of 1891 when President Benjamin Harrison visited Salt Lake City. That the old antagonisms had not disappeared was made plain when anti-Mormon public officials took over President Harrison and his party and endeavored to keep them from seeing conditions as they existed, particularly since the fraudulent elections of the previous year had placed the "carpet baggers" in control of local government. But the President of the United States showed his awareness of the facts and gave evidence of the change in official attitude when he, in James' words, "went far out of his way to announce his determination of dealing severely with certain classes of this community."

The President's visit on May 10 was one of the last public events in Salt Lake City in which Professor Talmage participated before leaving for Europe to attend the meetings of the Royal Microscopical Society. On May 22 he was set apart for the journey by Apostle Abraham H. Cannon and Elder John Jaques. The traveler was given a rich blessing which remained graven in his mind: that he should find success in his relations with the learned men whom he would meet, and be the means of allaying prejudice toward the Latter-day Saint people; that he should also find success in securing genealogical records of departed relatives in his native land; and that he would be preserved from danger and evil and be brought safely home.

Two days later, on May 24, James boarded the train and began his first trip back to the homeland he had left sixteen years before.

# First Return to Europe

James E. Talmage marvelled at "the wonders of modern travel" as he sped through the awe-inspiring scenery of the Royal Gorge on the Salt Lake-Denver first leg of his journey back to the land of his birth.

"We sit on cushions of velvet, reclining at night on comfortable beds, while we are swept along at a mile a minute," he noted appreciatively. The train's dining car further impressed the traveler.

"Think of it," he wrote, "a hotel on wheels and a dinner 50 miles long!" Eighty years later, his grandchildren and great-grandchildren reacted in much the same way to jet speeds more than ten times that of the Denver and Rio Grande of 1891, and to meals that stretched from the Rocky Mountains to the great cities of the Midwest.

Railroad accommodations must by 1891 have improved substantially since James' earlier cross-country trips, when travelling appeared to have been something of an ordeal. However, part of the difference may have been in the attitude of the traveller. Undoubtedly he now could afford better accommodations, and his mind was free of the type of worries which had beset him as he went toward the strange experience of eastern college life with extremely limited funds to see him through. This time he was able to enjoy travel for its own sake.

James had two major objectives in making the trip to Europe; attendance at the meetings of the Royal Microscopical Society, of course; and the obtaining of family records from the Hungerford-Ramsbury area for purposes of temple work. However, the opportunities to revisit scenes of childhood, to renew old friendships, and to enjoy the pleasant and educational advantages of travel were also warmly welcomed.

On May 30 he boarded the good ship *Alaska* of the Gurion Line in New York harbor for the next stage of his journey. The *Alaska,* "a magnificent boat, where nothing has been spared in providing for the comfort of the passengers," afforded another impressive demonstration of the wonders of modern travel, but James' appreciation of the luxury was sharply tempered by bouts of acute seasickness which beset him throughout the crossing.

The *Alaska* cast anchor at Liverpool on June 7, and the seasick traveller gratefully felt the reassurance of solid earth under his feet again. The first requirement after landing was to pass through customs inspection, and here Professor Talmage gave vent to one of his rare shows of resentment for petty officiousness.

The customs inspector was a most sarcastic man, and perhaps he was in a bad humor for personal reasons. Whatever the cause, his actions were maddeningly slow and often deliberately offensive. Dr. Talmage, his baggage waiting in the "T" section, had a disagreeably long wait but bore it with fortitude, having carefully filled out the customs declaration form.

When at last the inspector reached the waiting professor, the official snatched the declaration held out to him, glanced rapidly over it, and said accusingly:

"But you have declared nothing dutiable."

"I believe I have nothing dutiable to declare," the traveller replied calmly.

"Come, come, my man, *everyone* has something to declare!" the inspector said with a show of indignation, as though he had received a personal affront. "Personal effects, jewelry, liquor, tobacco . . . they're all dutiable."

Professor Talmage, his patience worn thin, kept his outward composure and replied in a level voice: "I don't carry expensive jewelry and it so happens that I don't smoke and

I don't drink liquor. I believe my declaration has been accurately filled out and that I have nothing at all to declare."

The customs inspector snorted disdainfully and proceeded to give the professor's luggage a most thorough examination. He would show this ignorant American, and all the other waiting boat passengers, that *every traveller* has *something* dutiable to declare.

Now Dr. Talmage had come prepared to be something more than a mere spectator at the forthcoming meeting of the Royal Microscopical Society. In case he, as a new member and coming from a far country, should be called on for a contribution to the proceedings, he had written a short paper on the Great Salt Lake and the surrounding desert. For illustration, he had brought a sample of the lake water containing the tiny *artemis fertilis,* or brine shrimp, only animal form able to live in the lake water, and three horned lizards, commonly called "hornéd toads," as illustrative of animal life on the desert shore. Though a non-smoker and non-drinker as he had informed the customs inspector, Professor Talmage was acquainted with men who indulged in both practices, and had secured a cigar box and a flat pint whiskey bottle as convenient carriers for his exotic fauna. The customs inspector had barely started his thorough search of the professor's baggage when he encountered the cigar box.

"Ha!" he cried triumphantly, holding the box aloft for all to see. "I thought you said you were carrying no tobacco."

"No, no tobacco," Dr. Talmage replied quietly, and offered no further comment.

"We'll see what you Americans are smoking these days in place of tobacco," the inspector said with a wink to the crowd which had gathered around. He opened the box.

Most Westerners have sometime seen a "hornéd toad," a perfectly harmless but poisonous-looking little creature, whose appearance is bound to be alarming to anyone seeing it for the first time. One of the lizards promptly jumped from the box in which it had been so long confined onto the inspector's hand.

The official, in near-panic, leaped backward and tripped over a piece of baggage. Professor Talmage retrieved the lizard and returned it to the box while the embarrassed customs official arose red-faced, fuming with anger, and gingerly rubbing assorted sore spots on his anatomy. Most of the spectators, thoroughly annoyed with the inspector's petty officiousness, were openly laughing, adding to the official's mounting rage.

He said no more but grimly set about a further search of Professor Talmage's luggage, determined to find some dutiable object—and *then* this upstart American would taste the full severity of British law. Articles of clothing were recklessly flung about, but Dr. Talmage kept his studied composure. He perceived a vague possibility which was becoming less vague by the moment. Hopefully he awaited the almost inevitable next act in the little farce.

He did not have long to wait. The inspector encountered, carefully wrapped in layers of clothing for protection against breakage—although in the outraged official's eyes it seemed obviously for purposes of concealment—a pint bottle of the size and shape traditionally used to contain whiskey. Holding it to the light he could see it was filled with liquid. The colored glass of the bottle prevented any exact determination of the nature of the liquid. But the inspector was certain he had what he wanted.

"I thought you said you had no liquor," he said fiercely, holding the bottle up for dramatic effect.

"No liquor," Dr. Talmage said laconically. The vague possibility had now become a virtual certainty, but he took no action to interfere.

"We'll *see* what you Americans are drinking instead of whiskey," the inspector said scornfully, and he uncapped the bottle and put it to his lips.

Everyone who has ever bathed in the Great Salt Lake has at some time accidentally taken a mouthful of water, and knows the unpleasantness of swallowing even the tiniest amount of the supersaturated brine. The shock of quaffing deeply, even greedily, of the lake water in the belief that it is a choice liquor may well be imagined. The customs inspector gasped, choked, coughed, and spat as he flopped about the customs shed in agony, undoubtedly thinking that he was literally strangling and that the end might come any moment.

Dr. Talmage had alertly taken the bottle from the inspector's hand lest it be broken and its scientifically-precious contents lost. He then sat quietly by as the stricken inspector went through his agonized contortions, saying nothing except to assure awed fellow passengers that the bottle contained no poison, but merely the over-salty water from the far-off Great Salt Lake.

The inspector's next act was awaited with hushed interest, as the anticipated explosion of personal temper and official ire might well be of historic proportions. But the customs official was through. He made one last attempt to assert his authority, but it failed miserably. When he tried to glare angrily, his watering eyes only rolled weakly in their sockets and closed tight in pain. When he tried to roar authoritatively he could only manage a hoarse croak.

In desperation, the inspector grabbed a piece of chalk and marked each piece of the professor's baggage to show that it had passed inspection. Pausing for a brief moment, he then suddenly turned and moved rapidly about the shed, marking *all* items of uninspected luggage. After that, he dashed out of the door and disappeared from the view of the ship's passengers, possibly in search of a bottle whose contents could be trusted to match their container.

In later years, Dr. Talmage would say, mock-seriously, that he had no idea how many professional smugglers he may have provided with a free pass through British customs on this occasion.

The return to his native land after sixteen years rekindled many memories in Professor Talmage's mind. It also opened his eyes to conditions which he had forgotten, or of which he had not been aware when he passed through the great port city of Liverpool as a boy of thirteen. The extent and frightfulness of the slums surpassed even those which had so shocked and depressed him in Baltimore, and almost numbed his mind. Most impressive and depressing of all were the hundreds, perhaps thousands, of prostitutes whom he saw openly plying their trade over wide areas of the city, including streets within sight of the front door of British and European Mission headquarters at 42 Islington. A few days later he took horrified note of similar situations in London and especially in the fashionable West End areas. The spectacle presented nightly in and around Piccadilly Circus was almost beyond the belief of the visitor from Utah who had been born a citizen of this island country.

"They were all well dressed," he said of the women of the West End streets. "Indeed, the display of fine clothing was remarkable. Most of the women were good looking, many of them decidedly handsome—indeed, it would appear that a plain or poorly dressed girl would stand little chance of success in the fierce competition of this unholy trade."

Sight of the men for whose custom the street walkers were competing was equally shocking.

"They were there, of all ages and qualities—boys and greybeards, most of them well attired and apparently well-to-do," Dr. Talmage wrote. "There were 'swells,' including officers of the army, and no attempt was made to effect disguises. There were students in their college caps, and even *ministers* of the Gospel of Christ (self-professed), their dress betraying them. We saw one of this class led off by a young girl—to perdition!"

That these conditions should be casually accepted by British society was deeply shocking. But the crown to this incredible hypocrisy was the almost universal attitude of Britons to the "Mormons"—who were rejected, condemned, and persecuted on the pretense that they were immoral.

Professor Talmage's reaction to his native land was not all negative. While shocked and disgusted by the immorality and saddened by the misery he encountered in the sprawling slums of Liverpool and the fashionable streets of London, he was thrilled and uplifted by the many beautiful and admirable things which he saw. The lovely parks and gardens, open to all, were an aesthetic delight. The botanical and zoological collections were fascinating both to the casual visitor and to one of scientific bent. The British Museum was a never-ending source of pleasant and profitable study, and Dr. Talmage visited it again and again. The English countryside, almost too green to be true, sprinkled with stately trees and colorful flowers, and at its glorious best in June, was a pure delight as he travelled through it.

As time permitted, Professor Talmage met with the missionary Elders wherever he might be. He spoke at open-air or "street" meetings, at cottage meetings, and in regular Sunday services, and otherwise participated in missionary labors.

On June 12, Dr. Talmage first went to the "rooms" of the Royal Microscopical Society at 20 Hanover Square in London, to make himself known and become acquainted with the locale. He was kindly received and shown through the Society's treasures. At the official annual meeting of the Society on the evening of June 17, Dr. Talmage expected merely to be recognized as a new member, but found himself called upon to address the gathering. He did so, discussing "the scientific wealth yet unmined in the land of my home," with special emphasis on the Great Salt Lake. Professor Talmage's microscopic slides of the *artemis fertilis* (brine shrimp) and oolitic (spherical) sand were viewed with interest as were the live shrimp which had escaped the greedy gulping of the customs official. The hornéd lizards had their moment in the limelight, and later found a permanent home in the zoological gardens of Regent's Park and the South Kensington Natural History Museum, a branch of the British Museum.

In his room that night after the Society's meeting was over, James reviewed in his mind the impressive event, and returned thanks to the Lord for the privilege he had been accorded in attending.

"I regard the occurrences of this night as very significant," he wrote in his journal, "not because *I* have gained recog-

James E. Talmage dons academic cap and gown for the ceremony of his installation as a Fellow of the Royal Microscopical Society, London, 1891. Inset shows a micro-photo of the brine shrimp *(artemis fertilis)* from the Great Salt Lake which were featured in the paper Professor Talmage presented before the Society—and which figured informally and more spectacularly during the customs inspection at the British port of entry.

nition in so august a society, but because a representative of
the Latter-day Saint Church—one of the despised 'Mormons'
—has been so received."

Having attained the first objective of his seven-thousand-
mile trip, James turned his full attention to the second: a
return to his boyhood home and the search for genealogical
records.

The "looking up" of relatives actually had begun earlier.
While in Liverpool, before going down to London, James had
made an excursion to Leigh, Lancashire, to call on Mrs.
Alice Ditchfield, an aunt of his wife. Mrs. Ditchfield, "a
good-hearted Lancashire lass of 76 years," welcomed him
warmly, recognizing him instantly from pictures that had been
enclosed in letters from her niece May. The elderly English-
woman introduced James to her friends and neighbors, all
of whom received him in the most friendly fashion, although
they were filled with strange ideas concerning Utah and the
Mormons. James did his best to correct their false ideas and
remove their prejudices.

When James later went to Hungerford and Ramsbury to
visit his own blood relatives and former neighbors, he met a
less cordial initial reception. Evidently there had been some
strong feelings about the Talmage family's emigration to Utah,
and it had not entirely died down. Before James concluded
his visit, friendly relations were re-established between himself
and his many Berkshire and Wiltshire relatives, but at the
outset there existed a noticeable air of constraint.

James arrived in Hungerford late in the evening of June
22 and sought quarters in the Bell Hotel, once operated by
his father, but the place was full, as were other public hostel-
ries in the town. He eventually called upon, and was invited
to stay with, the William Harris family, next-door neighbors
in the old days, whose warmth of greeting and all-out friend-
liness surprised the visitor.

James found that his cousins' views on Mormonism were
not the only things which had not changed since he left
Hungerford, sixteen years previously.

"Everything looks as it used to," he noted after his first 1891 stroll about the town. "There are the same houses— I didn't find a new one. There are the same shops, the same shopkeepers—everything the same. What a contrast with the ever-shifting, ever-improving conditions of our new country!"

Going from Hungerford to Ramsbury, James found himself riding in the same ancient carrier van in which he had ridden more than 20 years before when he was a schoolboy.

"The van even had the same driver—good old 'Dick' Chamberlain, as he is familiarly called," James noted with delight. "And he tells me it is the same horse and the same harness. The old man stopped at the same public houses as of old, and for the self-same purpose."

Although James took pride in the spirit of progress of his adopted country as contrasted with the changelessness of his native land, he found a great thrill of excitement and nostalgic affection as his eyes rested again on the old familiar sights and he mingled again with people he had known in boyhood days.

"I seemed to remember the whole road; could locate the trees and milestones, the hedges and the houses," he wrote in obvious joy of his first ride from Hungerford to Ramsbury. James' heart "throbbed wildly" as he retraced the old paths and visited places which held so many deeply personal memories from the days of childhood, life's most impressionable. When he walked the banks of the canal where he used to fish and found a lad there a-fishing, he hired the boy's tackle for a brief spell and, luck smiling upon him, caught five fine perch which he gave to the boy, along with "threepence" for the use of the tackle. (It was on a later occasion that James fished these same waters in exact fulfillment of his expressed desire to fish "as I used to do"—staying hour after hour at the waterside, catching nothing.)

On reaching Ramsbury, James' first visit was to the grave of his grandfather. He plucked forget-me-nots and daisies from the profusion of simple flowers growing on the grave and later enclosed them in a letter to his father and mother.

Soon, however, he was visiting the living, relatives and friends, and finally Mr. Newhook, the schoolmaster who had once so scorned the Mormons and had administered so many canings to the young Latter-day Saint who had been his pupil and who had fiercely upheld his unpopular beliefs.

On this occasion, Mr. Newhook received James gladly, amazed that the latter not only had come back from far-off, sinister Utah, but had come back to receive honors from English institutions of high repute. The schoolmaster—and he still retained that position—showed his visitor through the school and with considerable pride introduced the former pupil to those of the present day, and sent for Mrs. Newhook to come from home to the school to add to the welcome. Later, Professor Talmage was invited to the Newhook home for a long evening including not just one but two dinners: the regular evening meal at 5 o'clock and a substantial supper at 10. James wondered "how these good English people can possibly eat so often," but was happy to spend so many hours in the home of his old schoolmaster. He was able to correct a host of false beliefs which Mr. Newhook still held concerning Utah and the Latter-day Saints—which, James had heard, Mr. Newhook had continued to impart to his pupils whenever occasion offered.

Mr. Newhook must have been considerably impressed by the long discussion on the realities concerning Utah and its people, for the following day, when Dr. Talmage joined him in attending services at Saviour's Church, Eddington, the schoolmaster took his one-time pupil to meet "all the prominent men he could find," presenting him as "President of a Mormon College and a Fellow of our famous Microscopical Society."

After his arrival in the Hungerford-Ramsbury area, James lost little time in getting down to the basic purpose of his visit, the securing of genealogical records.

The first day of examining the records in Ramsbury, James was able to find and copy 22 entries of the Talmage family, dating from 1699 to 1810. One interesting discovery

James Newhook, James E. Talmage's schoolmaster in boyhood days in Hungerford. Mr. Newhook roundly denounced the Mormons at that time, but was proud to claim acquaintance with his erstwhile Mormon pupil when James returned to accept scientific recognition and honors in his native land.

which he made was the variation in the spelling of the family name over the years. He had noted that the people of Wiltshire of the day pronounced "Talmage" as if it were spelled "Tammage," and he found that in 1714 the name appeared in the parish register as "Tamidge." In 1708-9 it was spelled "Tamage," and back in 1699 it had been "Tammage." James later consulted the noted British genealogist, Henry Gray, who researched the question and informed James that the early British family names Talmach, Talmash, Talmache, and Tollemacke appeared to be related in medieval times, and that Talmage directly traced from the last of those listed.

Additional studies were made of the records at Hungerford, and at nearby Lambourne, ancestral village of the Preater family from which James' mother came. Before leaving the area, James obtained a substantial volume of invaluable genealogical records.

Later, just before sailing for home in August, Dr. Talmage spent a day in the genealogical section of the British Museum Library and found evidence to confirm Mr. Gray's opinions. He further discovered that a branch of the family had been prominent in Scotland, the "Talmaches" having at one time been the Earls of Dysart.

On his last Sunday in Ramsbury, Dr. Talmage delivered an address on "Utah and the Mormons" at the public hall. Handbills were distributed to advertise the appearance of "Dr. J. E. Talmage, formerly of Ramsbury, Wilts, now of Salt Lake City, Utah, USA." The public hall was filled to capacity, and James was deeply grateful for the opportunity to tell the story of Mormonism, and bear his testimony of its veracity, to his former friends and neighbors.

The effectiveness of James' efforts to dispel the misconceptions of the local people concerning the Latter-day Saints was most clearly shown as the time for departure arrived. His cousins, the Pullens, the Hackers, the Rosiers, the Shephards, the Franklins, the Kimbers, and the Talmages, none of whom had offered him lodging in their homes on his arrival, openly confessed their shame and warmly invited him to stay with them on any future visit. Mrs. Pullen tearfully confessed that, when she had first received word that her Mormon cousin from Utah was coming to Ramsbury, she had vehemently declared that she would not meet him, not "soil her hands by contact with those of a Mormon." She earnestly begged forgiveness and entreated James on any future return to Ramsbury to make her house his home.

James left his boyhood home with many fond memories of the visit, and nostalgic thoughts of the now-distant boyhood experiences. But he was sharply reminded of the contrast of the way of life he had left and that to which he had gone. During his final days in Ramsbury he had roomed and boarded with a Mr. Jones, a good-hearted, friendly man of 67, who earned his living working on a farm four miles from town.

Mr. Jones arose each morning at 2:30, walked the four miles and began the day's work at 4 A.M. He walked home again in the evening, arriving at 6:30 to eat an austere supper and fall into bed for an all-too-brief night's sleep. The old man saw nothing unusual in his situation and accepted it cheerfully.

Shortly after returning to London near the end of June, Professor Talmage joined Reed Smoot and Samuel King, recently released missionaries, to plan and undertake a tour on the European continent. They made their travel arrangements through the already-famous firm of Thomas Cook & Sons and made the "Cook's Tour" which has become a part of the language.

All three travellers enjoyed their trip immensely, visiting Belgium, the Netherlands, Germany, Switzerland, Italy, and France before returning to Britain and taking passage home. Professor Talmage was impressed with all that he saw, the beautiful and occasionally the ugly, the customs and the institutions, the people and their attitudes. He rhapsodized over the awe-inspiring beauty, both natural and man-made, and was frequently reminded of passages of the poets, describing what he was now seeing and emotions which they invoked in his own breast as in those of earlier viewers.

Paintings, sculpture, and architecture were deeply appreciated and praised; yet the wonders of nature—the magnificent Alps, the glaciers at Chamonix, the fiery Vesuvius and the awesome evidence of its devastating power centuries ago, in buried Pompeii and Herculanum—impressed the scientist and teacher in a different way. *These* were things he understood in depth, and his inner excitement on being able to examine them at close range is clearly discernible in his journal writings in contrast to the calmer admiration he accorded great works of art, for example, on which he looked only as a deeply stirred spectator.

The three travellers returned to London for a few days in early August, before proceeding to Liverpool and boarding the SS *Alaska*—the same vessel in which Dr. Talmage had made the west-east crossing in June. Other Utahns were aboard the *Alaska*—John McEwan, the noted actor Phil Margetts, and Professor Talmage's room-mate, Elder James Wardrops, who was forced by ill health to return home after serving only a few weeks in the mission field.

The passage was a stormy one and seasickness was rife, but the ship made good time, arriving at Sandy Hook on August 16.

With only a brief pause in the East, largely for the purpose of ordering scientific supplies for the College from James Green and Co. in Philadelphia, Dr. Talmage hurried West, arriving in Salt Lake City on August 22.

# Developing Plans

After a three-month absence from home, Dr. Talmage returned full of pent-up enthusiasm and energy for his professional labors at the College and the Deseret Museum.

There were exciting prospects of change in the direction of progress and expansion, a move to new and more convenient quarters for both institutions. Plans were being formed and considered for basic changes in the Church educational system, changes which might effect corresponding alterations in Professor Talmage's lifetime career.

There were to be changes, indeed, with far-reaching effects both on the course of the Church school program and on the private destinies of James E. Talmage. Some were anticipated, but the most significant were unsuspected at this time and stemmed largely from the adverse economic conditions which were developing across the nation. There were also more pleasant surprises in store in Professor Talmage's personal career.

The new quarters which had been secured for the College consisted of a large private dwelling on West First North, which was extensively remodelled to adapt it to its new use. It was far from perfectly suited to its purpose, but a marked improvement over the old quarters in historic Social Hall. The move did not herald major growth in the institution, for it could accommodate only about the same number of students as were already in attendance, but these could be made more comfortable. Quantities of new technical and scientific equipment had been installed, and Dr. Talmage noted that his own laboratory was "the most convenient [private] laboratory it has ever been my privilege to work in."

Hardly were the College and its president settled in their new quarters, however, than indications of imminent and extensive change in their relationship appeared. On December 30, 1891, a meeting of the Church Board of Education was held for the purpose of discussing the founding of a Church University which would be a university in fact and not just an expansion of one of the existing academies or colleges. The Board expressed its collective desire to have Professor Talmage released from his position as president of the College to devote a substantial part of his time to making preparations for the proposed new institution, which would be named Young University. He was to work with Captain Willard Young as a committee of two in the initial stages of the program.

The proposal to remove Dr. Talmage from the presidency of LDS College at first met with strong resistance from the Board of Education of Salt Lake Stake, supervisory body of the College. They particularly objected to making the change in the middle of an academic year, and expressed fears that such action would both disrupt the smooth operation of the relatively young institution and also deter the further enrollment of students. For a time the argument waxed warm, but it soon reached its virtually inevitable conclusion: the will of the board with higher authority prevailed.

James E. Talmage himself was torn by mixed emotions. He was deeply involved in the affairs of the College which he had guided through its early, problem-set years. He was joyfully looking forward to the expanded opportunities afforded by the new quarters and to further growth and expansion in the future. Yet he was deeply stirred by the prospect of the founding of a genuine Church University, an institution of wide scope and high standards that would merit recognition by the established centers of learning throughout the nation and the world. It was a dream he had cherished for many years.

As for his own dissociation with the College, he felt personal regrets, but was less concerned about the possible adverse results on the institution than were the Stake Board members who were so vigorously protesting the proposed move. "Students and patrons will discover that with the College, as with all other institutions of the Church, success of such an institution depends not on Brother Talmage or on any other man," he wrote. "By the close of the school year, any signs of disappointment will have been lived down and students will leave with feelings of confidence and will reenter with redoubled energy."

Little time was lost in carrying out the decision of the Church Board, once the initial objections of the College Board had been considered and given reply. On January 11, 1892, Dr. Talmage was officially released from his duties as principal of the College and Professor Willard Done, his long-time, highly valued and esteemed assistant, was named to replace him.

Professor Talmage was also released from "all normal, theological and executive duties in the College," according to the published announcement, but would "continue his scientific lectures before the students until the close of the present academic year."

Dr. Talmage quickly found the new arrangement to be to his liking. Relieved of the time-consuming details of administrative work, he was able to devote more time to the preparation of his scientific classes at the College, and he felt that their quality improved accordingly. He was imbued with the true missionary zeal in his labors toward the establishment of the proposed Young University, and he was also given more time to devote to his duties as curator of the Deseret Museum, which within two years achieved international recognition.

In the matter of salary, the Church Board of Education decided that the same remuneration, $200 a month, which Professor Talmage had received as principal of the College should continue to be paid him, but warned that an even smaller percentage than before was to be expected in cash, the remainder coming in "Church pay"—i.e., orders for food and other items at the Tithing Office. James was not greatly troubled by the fact that he would receive relatively little of his salary in cash, so long as he did receive it. A short time previously, in December 1891, before his transfer from the College had been proposed, he had discussed with the Church Board of Education the plight of his teachers who, in common with other employees of Church institutions had not received their cash salaries for an extended period. He was himself in like situation, of course, but noted that "this troubles me little, provided I can get enough means to keep up my dues [in scientific organizations] and live out of debt."

A few days after making this observation, on December 21, James had his family obligations added to by the arrival of a second child, another son, given the name of Paul Booth Talmage. James and May greatly rejoiced, and never once thought of the new arrival as adding to their financial problems. They owned their own modest home and had no rent to pay; the "tithing scrip" provided food enough and.other absolute necessities, and they carefully husbanded the little money that came from time to time and were content, strong in their faith that the Lord would provide if they did their own part.

Perhaps the most remarkable aspect of the situation through the financially difficult years is that James was able, while always keeping out of debt and maintaining his family in reasonable comfort, to embark on periodic trips abroad to attend the meetings of scientific organizations and make special studies. These were always undertaken with the full approval—the definite urging, actually—of the First Presidency of the Church, and what financial assistance was possible was provided, but the major burden fell on the young professor and his own straitened means. The Church itself was in almost as great difficulty as the poorest of its members through this very difficult period of its history.

Still more stringent times lay ahead for the little Talmage family, had they but known it. Yet had they known the full detail, it is unlikely that they would have been greatly troubled, for when the most difficult times arrived they were met with the same calm spirit and unshakable faith evidenced earlier.

Just two years later, on Christmas Day 1893, when the full force of the financial "panic" was everywhere felt with devastating effect, particularly on the Church plans for an expanded school system, James noted in his private journal:

> A good wife is among the choicest jewels of man's life and though such ought to be prized at all times and under all circumstances, there are conditions that magnify her value. During the present tryingly stringent season in matters financial, many people have been loud in proclaiming their distress. As for ourselves, we have endured deprivation to as great an extent as most people are called to do except those who are suffering in abject poverty; for money has become to us almost an unknown quantity. All that I have received in salary account for many months has been in Tithing Scrip; and yet I have heard no word of complaint, and indeed little else than expressions of thankfulness in this regard at home. Wife has often remarked that if none suffer more than we do through hard times, there will be nothing serious. Still she has nobly sustained me in a position of safety—what we cannot obtain with the means at our disposal, we do without; and today, as indeed ever since the payment for our little home was completed, we are and have been, free of debt.
>
> But, by special kindness of the brethren in charge, I received a very few dollars in cash for the Christmas season; and today after enjoying a sumptuous feast, Maia surprised me by saying that all had been provided without the expenditure of a dollar in cash. Then, by closer examination, I found that the little cash received had been used for charitable purposes only, providing something for some of those she had discovered to be actually in want.
>
> A wife who can so manage and work is a gift from God.

Distressing times through which the people of Utah passed in this epoch were not caused solely by financial difficulties. Serious illness, of epidemic proportions, swept the territory and large numbers fell victim to La Grippe, which had recently ravaged much of Western Europe, and to diphtheria. It became not at all unusual for James to be called out a half-dozen to a dozen times a day—and night—to join with other priesthood holders in administering to the sick.

In those days, when hospitals were few and meagrely equipped, by today's standards, when doctors were fewer and medical knowledge so much less extensive than it would become over the ensuing decades, Latter-day Saints called on the Lord more frequently if not more fervently than they do in the late Twentieth Century. It was not uncommon for the priesthood to administer to a critically ill person several times in the course of the same day. The saints did not neglect the admonition to do what they could for themselves, and those who were well labored diligently and often to the point of physical exhaustion to care for the sick, using every scrap of knowledge and experience at their command. When a serious epidemic struck a community everyone was affected: the sparse corps of medically trained personnel, the devoted and compassionate women who retained the pioneer spirit, the holders of the priesthood—all were deeply involved in one way or another, and often an individual's activities were in more than one area.

An experience illustrative of the times, calling for personal effort and risk as well as prayer from the very bottom of the heart, came to James E. Talmage in the spring of 1892 when the ravages of diphtheria were at their terrible height in the territory. It involved a family of strangers, not members of the Church, who lived near the Talmage home.

Returning home from calling on a sick person on Memorial Day, a legal holiday free from regular duties, James learned of the terrible suffering and destitution of the family, Martin by name, which was stricken by diphtheria and without help. Ward Relief Society officers had been unable to find anyone willing to go to the pest-stricken house. Fear of the dreadful disease had reached panic proportions, and people—especially those with children—would not knowingly expose themselves to the germs.

When he heard of the Martins' plight, James immediately changed clothes and proceeded to their home, where he "found to exist a pitiful state of affairs."

> One child, two and a half years old, lay dead on a bed, having been dead about four hours and still unwashed. Two other children, one a boy of ten and the other a girl of five, lay writhing in the agonies of the disease. A girl of 13 years is still feeble from a recent attack of diphtheria. . . . The father, Mr. Abe Martin, and the mother, Marshia Martin, are dazed with grief and fatigue; and the only other occupant of the house, a man named Kelly who is a boarder in the family, is so ill and weak as hardly to be able to move about.

The siege of illness had gone on so long that the entire house was in a state of utter filth. After administering to the children at the request of the parents, James attacked the physical tasks, washing and laying out the little corpse, bathing the living children and clothing them in clean things sent in by the Relief Society. Food had also been sent in. Carpets were torn up, rooms swept, soiled clothing carried out, and the accumulation of filthy rags burned.

While James was at work, a woman came to the door, a stranger, offering to help for a consideration of $5 a day, a very high wage for those days. Told of the family's utter destitution, the woman lowered her price to $4.50. James' soul was revolted and he "told her to go, not to stay in the house of poverty, suffering, and death and act the vulture." He assured the Martin family that they would not be without help, that he would stay with them if other assistance could not be found.

He worked through the day, and someone was found to come in and sit as a night watch. Before leaving for the night, James and Bishop Hardy, who came by especially, again administered to the sick.

Returning next morning, James learned that the ten-year-old boy had died during the night, and found the little girl of five apparently in her last agonies. He took her in his arms and did his best to comfort her.

"She clung to my neck," he related, "ofttimes coughing bloody mucus on my face and clothing, and her throat had about it the stench of putrefaction, yet I could not put her from me. During the half hour immediately preceding her death, I walked the floor with the little creature in my arms. She died in agony at 10 A.M."

Under the harsh regulations of the plague-stricken time, an undertaker was called immediately, the three little corpses were placed in wooden coffins and taken to the cemetery without delay. They were buried in a single grave and "the grief of the parents and the surviving sister were pitiable to behold." James delivered a brief graveside talk and Bishop Hardy pronounced a dedicatory prayer.

After making arrangements for food and clean clothing to be taken to the Martins'—survivors had experienced the dread diphtheria and so were immune to further attack— James went home. He changed clothes and bathed "in a strong zinc solution, in the coal house" and kept away from the rest of the family for a considerable period.

The emotional and physical strain of such an experience may be imagined. Fear that the dread disease might have taken deep root in his own person, or that he might serve as carrier to transmit the deadly germs to his own loved ones, must have been all but overpowering; yet it is referred to only obliquely. The day following his return home, James' journal entry consisted of a terse comment:

"Confined to the house the entire day through illness— fever, lassitude, and pains in the head. All temporary, I hope —simply the effect of over-exertion and nervous strain, I think."

By the grace of the Almighty, such proved to be the case. Each succeeding day brought improvement until within a week he was physically fully restored. The emotional impact, the heart-rending suffering and grief which he had witnessed, remained deeply etched in his mind, never to be effaced.

In the summer of 1892 James was commissioned by the First Presidency to go into the colorful desert country of Southeastern Utah to examine a number of reported archaeological discoveries, particularly purported Indian writings on the rocks, which were said to be of exceptional interest.

The trip was completely negative as regards its primary purpose. The "Indian hieroglyphics" proved to be crude forgeries of obvious recent execution, or, in some cases, actually non-existent: figments of the distorted imagination of the man who had reported the "finds" and who was found to be mentally unbalanced.

The rugged and physically taxing journey proved to be more than worth while, however, for another reason.

Professor Talmage made a side-excursion from Loa, Wayne County, to the southeast into the area now designated as Capitol Reef National Park, to examine an unusual deposit of the mineral selenite which was reported to him by some of the local people. The selenite geode, unlike the reported "Indian hieroglyphics," proved anything but a disappointment. It was deeply impressive to the geologist on first sight, and proved to be one of the outstanding selenite deposits in the world.

Selenite is a variation of the mineral gypsum, of little commercial value, but great scientific interest. In its pure form, selenite has colorless transparency to rival glass. Its crystalline structure and the property of breaking into perfectly regular, flat sheets, gives it unusual interest to geologists and mineralogists. The magnificent deposit in a wash some $3\frac{1}{2}$ miles above the Dirty Devil River, which Dr. Talmage saw on April 12, 1892, provided specimens which eventually found their way into museums and institutions of learning over much of the Western world. It provided a medium of exchange by which the Deseret Museum was able to secure a wide variety of outstanding specimens from many of the great museums of Europe and North America and made the name of the Utah institution known in scientific circles far and near. In the late Twentieth Century, the Utah selenite deposit is still cited in reference books as one of the outstanding discoveries of this mineral.

Early in 1893, optimism toward the economic outlook still prevailed and it was decided that Dr. Talmage should return to Europe, specifically to take selenite specimens to the major museums and personally to select suitable exchange items to be placed in the Deseret Museum. Correspondence had already been opened with many of the institutions, which had evidenced a keen interest in making such exchanges on the basis of the reports of the characteristics of the Utah selenite. While in Europe Dr. Talmage would, of course, attend meetings of scientific societies, including that of the Museum Association, to which it was hoped to obtain membership for the Deseret Museum.

The European trip was highly successful in fulfilling its basic purpose of placing the Utah selenite in prominent museums and institutions, and obtaining from them valuable exchange specimens. The trip also had an important bearing on the personal career of James E. Talmage.

Presentations of the mineral, accompanied by photographs of the geode in its original state, were made to the Royal Society of Edinburgh, the South Kensington Natural History Museum (a branch of the British Museum), the museums of Cambridge and Oxford Universities, the Museum of Practical Geology in London, the international Museum Association, and the Institute of France, in Paris. In addition, a special presentation was of course made to the Royal Microscopical Society when James attended its annual meeting, and 150 small specimens were individually packaged and presented, one to each of the Society's members, to their great delight.

The reception accorded the spectacular mineral exhibits by these world-renowned institutions was impressive, and fully justified the considerable time and effort that had gone into their preparation and Dr. Talmage's 7,000-mile journey.

At the meeting of the Royal Society of Edinburgh, the selenite specimens and photographs were prominently displayed on a table in the center of the meeting room. The chairman, Lord M'Laren, called on the visitor from Utah for an unscheduled address and the regular agenda was interrupted for a general discussion of the selenite discovery.

So impressive was the reception given the Utah selenite that another trip to Europe was made in 1894, for the purpose of placing selenite exhibits in major museums on the Continent of Europe, most notably the *Museum für Naturkünde* of Berlin University, which housed what were then generally recognized as the outstanding selenite specimens in the world.

German museum officials were coldly reserved in the initial reception of Dr. Talmage when they learned the purpose of his visit, but the reserve was transformed into excited enthusiasm when they saw the minerals he had brought, which far outshone their own prized exhibits.

On his trip to Edinburgh to make the presentation to the Royal Society of Edinburgh, in 1893, James made contacts that were of lasting significance in his personal life and career. In making arrangements for the mineral presentation, James met Peter Guthrie Tait, professor of physics and natural philosophy at the University of Edinburgh and secretary of the Royal Society. Professor Tait introduced his American visitor to Professor James Giekie, the eminent geologist, and the three men of science immediately struck a chord of mutual understanding and admiration that ripened into lifelong friendship. Before he left Edinburgh, Dr. Talmage was astonished when Professors Tait and Giekie proposed to nominate him for membership in the Royal Society of Edinburgh.

The Utahn was taken to the University and subjected to a rigid examination by a panel of eminent men of science in case such nomination should be made, although a major obstacle was foreseen in a provision of the Society's charter restricting membership to British subjects. Dr. Talmage left Scotland with little expectation of further developments in this matter, although Professors Giekie and Tait expressed confidence that the obstacle could be surmounted.

# The "Panic of 1893" Changes Plans

James returned from Europe at the end of July, 1893, and found himself in an atmosphere very different from that he had felt on his departure from Utah three months previously. It was almost as though he had come back to a different world.

As soon as he reached the shores of the United States, and especially when he arrived in Utah, James was made aware of the full-scale impact of the historic financial panic of 1893. This was no local manifestation of hard times, but a national disaster. On July 31, the day following his return, he wrote:

> I find that the painful stringency in the money market is felt here in Utah as elsewhere, though the proverbial careful and conservative course of our people prevent such frequent failures as are reported elsewhere in the world. I have never known a stronger current of financial difficulty than seems now to have swept over the land.

Within a few days, the impact of the panic was felt by Dr. Talmage directly. On August 11, the Church Board of Education felt itself forced to adopt a most distasteful policy. Appropriations for the support of Church schools had to be temporarily stopped, and as a consequence some twenty of them had to close until the situation should improve. It was further reluctantly decided that the long and eagerly awaited opening of Young University, scheduled for the fall of 1893, would have to be postponed indefinitely, even though the building was nearly in readiness, and most of the equipment had been purchased and set up.

Later in the month, Professor Talmage presented and the Board adopted a plan to utilize to the greatest possible extent the facilities and apparatus that had already been obtained, without incurring substantial additional expense. Portions of the building and equipment which had been prepared for the anticipated opening of the Church University in Salt Lake would be placed at the disposal of LDS College. Professor Talmage would conduct classes in chemistry and natural philosophy, to be open without charge to all qualified students of the College, which would then be relieved of the need to conduct its own program. Two assistant teachers, for whom places had been established in the blueprint for the Church University operation but who had never been hired, would be dispensed with, and Professor Talmage would undertake all of the work except for the help that could be provided by the draftsman, clerk, and janitor who were already in the employment of the College.

This program put James back in the classroom—to his considerable satisfaction, for a part of his heart was always there. In fact, he carried a double load of classroom teaching through the 1893-94 academic year. Before leaving for Europe in the spring he had agreed to accept a limited assignment at the University of Utah, duties of which could be discharged concurrently with those of this position in the Church school system. In the fall of 1893, he began his labors as professor of metallurgy and biology, including classes in human physiology. The two teaching assignments, at the University and at the College, gave the professor a very full schedule, especially when he had to do the routine preparatory work at the College classroom without the help of trained assistants.

Effects of the stringent financial bind continued to grow in intensity and forced themselves onto everyone's attention in everyday walks of life. In late August, James took an over-all look at the distressing situation as it affected the nation, the local community, the Church, and himself. He wrote:

> From every side arises the cry of hard times. I have never witnessed a greater stagnation in business enterprises than has manifested itself during the last month. Money is not to be had,

confidence seems to have disappeared, and credit is denied to nearly all tradesmen. Public works are stopped and in this city alone thousands of men are out of employment. . . . Personally, I am keenly sensitive to the severity of the times; having absolutely no income but my monthly salary I feel any stoppage of the stream and for months I have been unable to draw a dollar in money. My journey to Europe reduced what little extra I had to almost nothing. Yet I rejoice that things are not worse and we feel that our family is particularly blessed. . . .

We have suspended all expenditures out of the ordinary, and defer as long as possible all but absolutely necessary purchases. But our chief blessing in these times lies in being out of debt. It is a rule with us never to go into debt, and since our modest home was paid for, we have had none.

James then summed up his personal review in a way that expressed his attitude toward life as well as toward the current crises:

"I feel that all will be well. I acknowledge the hand of God in present affairs and I look for great and good results.

"I am happy that the great Temple was completed before this financial crash. God willed it so."

Indeed, all Latter-day Saints took great comfort and pride in the glorious Temple, and those living in Salt Lake Valley rejoiced in the fact that they could do vicarious work for their dead regularly, close to home, without having to travel to Logan or Manti or St. George. James' journal entry reflected the thoughts of thousands in acknowledging the hand of the Lord in the timing that brought the Temple to completion before the full force of the financial crash struck the people.

When the capstone of the Temple had been set in place, on April 6, 1892, there had been impressive ceremonies and great rejoicing. The members of the Church had been called on to increase their already considerable sacrifices and efforts to hasten the final completion of the structure so that it might be dedicated one year thence, on April 6, 1893, sixty-third anniversary of the organization of the Church.

James had taken his appointed place as a holder of the priesthood and had been deeply thrilled as President Woodruff pressed an electrical control button which released a catch and let the topmost stone of the Temple fall into place. President Snow led the multitude of 40,000 in the solemn and sacred "Hosannah shout" which seemed to reverberate from the hills.

Elder Francis M. Lyman of the Council of the Twelve presented to the assembled throng a resolution, which was enthusiastically endorsed, by which the people pledged themselves, individually and collectively, to provide the means for finishing the Temple so that it could be dedicated one year later. Elder Lyman added example to precept by placing himself at the head of the list of donors to the special fund with a $1,000 donation. James pledged an amount equal (and in addition) to his full tithing and later in the year, in response to a renewed appeal from the Authorities, increased his total pledge by two-thirds. He did so with obvious joy and satisfaction, noting that "the Lord has blessed me greatly." His personal donation, modest in terms of actual dollars, was substantial in relation to his total income and large indeed in terms of the portion of his income which came in cash in these stringent times.

James' response to the appeal was typical of that of the saints throughout the territory, from the richest to the poorest, and the Temple Fund drive was completely successful in spite of the adverse conditions. The Temple was completed on schedule, and on April 6, 1893, the great edifice was dedicated in impressive ceremonies which were extended for many days, being repeated as many times as were necessary to allow all qualified Latter-day Saints to attend.

James was present at the first dedicatory ceremony, serving in the capacity of deacon in the administration of the sacrament and feeling deeply honored to have some part in the sacred and historic ceremony. He returned later with Maia and his parents and brother Albert in the allotted schedule for the wards—special arrangements having been made to allow them to attend as a family group.[1]

---

[1]More extensive descriptions of the Temple dedication are found in James E. Talmage's *The House of the Lord,* first published in 1912 and republished in 1962 by Bookcraft.

Through the dark days of economic depression, Latter-day Saints could and did take great pride in having completed the Temple before the worst of the financial panic and took comfort in being able to go frequently into the magnificent structure to labor for their dead. For many, whose standard of living had been drastically altered, it was about the only tangible comfort they had.

The Talmage family, as has been noted, felt no actual change in their way of daily life, but there can be no doubt that James' recently-acquired position on the University of Utah faculty must have been a real help through the winter of 1893-94 when remuneration for Church-connected activities was made entirely in "tithing scrip." The state-supported University of Utah was not, of course, above the reach of hard times, and indeed there were moments when its very existence hung in the balance.

In the winter of 1893-94, the University faced complications other than economic ones common to all the nation. Dr. John R. Park, first president of the institution, had resigned and the University was having to make its way through turbulent economic and political seas with temporary leadership.

James E. Talmage was aware that his name was frequently mentioned as a possible successor to Dr. Park, and he had received a number of informal "feelers" on the subject.

In late January, 1894, James was summoned by President Wilford Woodruff when Professors Joseph T. Kingsbury and William M. Stewart of the University called on the Church leader and proposed that Dr. Talmage be placed in the presidency of the institution and that the LDS Church and the State of Utah join forces, as it were, in order to maintain high quality education in the Territory in the face of the economic crisis. Salient points of the two professors' proposal were:

1. That the plan for founding a Church university be set aside for the present and that the Church throw its influence and support behind the territorial institution to develop a true university.

2. That with Dr. Talmage at its head, the University of Utah would be guaranteed against falling under the influence of the Church's enemies.

Presidents Woodruff and Smith took the matter under advisement, and the third member of the Presidency, President George Q. Cannon, who was in New York, was consulted by telegraph. Four days later, on January 29, President Woodruff called Professor Talmage to his office and told him of the decision that had been reached.

Plans for the Church university would be indefinitely suspended, and the influence of the Church would be placed behind the territorial institution. For the immediate future, the Church would concentrate its educational efforts on the development and improvement of the several stake academies, which were actually high schools, serving a function which was virtually unparalleled in the Utah public school system of that day. Dr. Talmage was therefore advised to accept the proffered University presidency, but on the express understanding that the institution would remain in Salt Lake City. Professors Kingsbury and Stewart were sent for and given this same message.

The insistence that the University remain in Salt Lake City was not a matter of casual thought or concern. The Territorial Legislature was in session, and the problem of financing the institutions of higher learning—the University of Utah and the Agricultural College in Logan—was acute in this time of financial crisis. Consolidation of the two colleges was being given serious consideration and the question of whether the combined institution should be located in Salt Lake or Logan was a major issue.

The future of both institutions was anything but assured, for the problem of adequate financial support loomed as menacingly large as ever. When the 1894 Legislature adjourned shortly afterward with the University's appropriation for the ensuing biennium set at just half the amount that had been appropriated in the previous fiscal period, Dr. Talmage met again with the First Presidency to review the Church's, and his own, position in the light of this development.

James' personal feelings were poured out in a journal entry on March 16, following the conference with the First Presidency. After noting that the ruling party in the legislature had apparently aimed to "doom [the University] to a slow death" he wondered if the Church should lend its influence and the names of its General Authorities to the support of a failing institution.

"Personally, I have never had a desire for the presidency of the institution, and I am loath to step on deck just in time to marshal all hands as the vessel goes down," he wrote. But his mood was not one of unmixed pessimism, for he went on to say:

> Did I think that the actions of the last Legislature represented the voice and wishes of the people, I should despair of the University's life; but I am convinced that the people have its interests at heart. The University of Utah, under the name of the University of Deseret, was founded by Latter-day Saints in the earliest days of the settlement of Utah, in the days of the people's direst poverty. I have faith that it will live.

It became clear that this last-expressed conviction overruled the doubts in James' mind for he did not withdraw his name from consideration. Nor did the First Presidency retract the offer to support the state university. On April 9 the University Board of Regents unanimously elected Dr. Talmage president of the institution and also confirmed his nomination for the newly-endowed Deseret Professorship of Geology.

The endowment of the Chair in geology was made by the Salt Lake Literary and Scientific Association, an LDS Church-affiliated group, and represented a measure of tangible support of the University to go along with the promised moral influence of the Church Authorities with the people in favor of the University. The endowment was in the sum of $60,000, one-fourth of which was paid by turning over to the University $15,000 worth of appropriate apparatus and material which had been acquired for use in the proposed Church university. Provision was made for the cash balance to be paid over a period of time, and until payment was completed the

Society contributed a pro rata portion of the incumbent's salary. The Society retained the right to nominate the occupant of the endowed chair.

Dr. Talmage accepted the initial appointment to the Deseret Chair of Geology, along with the presidency of the University, with mixed feelings. His chief regret was having to abandon chemistry as his scientific specialty, after the years of study and of teaching which he had devoted to it.

James also felt many misgivings and self-doubts in assuming the university presidency and the many attendant problems. The institution itself was in a state of turmoil as a result of disagreement between Dr. Park and some members of the faculty. Financial support of the institution was uncertain, as has been noted. In addition to these problems, there were still the strongly anti-Mormon elements that sought to take over control of the territory. Indeed, concern lest the University—founded and nurtured in its earliest days by the Latter-day Saints—should become a center of anti-Mormon influence, had been a major factor in the decision which had been made.

From the outset of Dr. Talmage's administration, there was no thought of making the University a Church institution, either openly or underground. The separation of Church and State was rigidly respected. Dr. Talmage himself, while remaining as dedicated a Church member and priesthood holder as ever in his strictly private life, forsook temporarily all public activity which would mark him as a leader in Church affairs. In this he acted not only in accordance with his own judgment but also on the counsel of the First Presidency. A series of special classes in Latter-day Saint theology which Dr. Talmage had been conducting for a period of many weeks, and which were to be the basis for the book *The Articles of Faith,* were abruptly terminated just prior to Dr. Talmage's accepting the university position.

Following the public announcement of Dr. Talmage's appointment to the University presidency, he half expected an expression of adverse criticism from the anti-Mormon element in the community. Happily, and somewhat surprisingly, it did not develop, at least not openly.

To the host of friends and well-wishers who hastened to offer congratulations, James expressed warm thanks but suggested that they withhold congratulations "until the new president had accomplished something to merit them."

# President of the University of Utah

The new president of the University quickly discovered that there would be no lack of opportunity to "accomplish something" to merit the congratulations—or draw the censure —of his friends. There was a great deal to be done.

Facing him from the outset was the residue of faculty turmoil which had been largely responsible for the change in leadership at the institution.[1]

The most pressing problem in 1894, however, was to obtain for the University maximum support from the community, moral as well as financial. To this end, Dr. Talmage met with the First Presidency of the Church within a week of his return, discussing with them the agreement under which the Church had laid aside its plan for immediate development of a Church university and was to throw its moral and material support behind the University of Utah.

Members of the Presidency responded promptly. On August 18, date of Dr. Talmage's first post-return extended interview with the Presidency, a letter was drafted which appeared over the names of the three members of the Presidency in the *Deseret News*. It set forth the basic reasons for delaying the establishment at this time of the previously-announced Church university, and called for members of the Church fully to support the territorial University in order to maintain and expand a quality institution of higher learning in the community.

---

[1] For more detail on the question of the dispute between Dr. Park and the University faculty, the reader is referred to published accounts such as: *The University of Utah: A History of Its First 100 Years—1850 to 1950,* by Ralph V. Chamberlin, University of Utah Press, 1960.

The Church leaders called on bishops of wards and presidents of stakes to have the letter read in their public gatherings and "to use their influence in otherwise bringing this subject before the people."

The letter was followed by an address by President George Q. Cannon at General Conference in October, going over essentially the same ground as the published letter, and the Presidency's position was sustained by vote of the assembly in the Tabernacle.

Church leaders lived up to their promise of material as well as moral support as best they could in the straitened times. Endowment of the Deseret Chair of Geology had been implemented by transferral to the University, for a credit of $15,000 against the $60,000 endowment, of the scientific apparatus which had been secured in anticipation of the planned Church institution. This was without doubt the finest, most up-to-date, and most complete collection of equipment for research and instruction in the physical sciences to be found in the Territory at this time and it was of great benefit to the University in the pursuance of its program of expansion and development.

Later, in March, 1896, the Church transferred to the University the new Deseret Museum Building on West First North, together with another smaller building and the full LDS College campus lot on which the buildings stood. The exchange was accepted by the University Regents in full payment of the remaining $45,000 of the endowment obligation, plus accrued interest to that date of $2,700, and the additional quarters were of inestimable value to the growing institution, pending later development of the new campus on the east bench adjacent to Fort Douglas.

Conditions at the University improved noticeably from those prevailing at the close of the previous academic year, when the faculty had been in conflict with the administration and some had left the institution. Morale improved greatly among those who remained when they found that changes were being effected in policies which they had resented and opposed, or at least were being given serious consideration. When the new president met with the Board of Regents on October 8, the first board meeting since he had taken office, he was pleased to be able to report that the institution was in a flourishing condition—in all aspects except financial. Enrollment had increased to the point where it had become necessary to add two instructors to the faculty, making seventeen in all; twenty-nine counting those engaged with the training school and with the School for the Deaf and Blind, which was then a part of the University. A spirit of unity and determination to succeed generally prevailed, replacing the disharmony, at times approaching open revolt, that had been prevalent the year before.

The one dark cloud on the otherwise bright scene—the fiscal outlook—was a matter of serious concern. The Territorial Legislature had appropriated $90,000 to operate the University through the academic years 1892-93 and 1893-94. Yet in spite of the fact that the growing institution was encountering financial problems—a 15 per cent salary cut had been imposed in March, 1894—the following Legislature had sliced the previous appropriation precisely in half: $45,000 to operate through the years 1894-95 and 1895-96.

Even the cut-in-half appropriation of $45,000 was not what it appeared to be on the surface. The institution had acquired a debt of $20,000 which had to be repaid, leaving only $25,000 for actual operation during the biennium. It was an impossible task, but by borrowing $16,000 from its land fund, calling on alumni and friends for all possible assistance, and tightening its belt to the last notch, the University managed not only to survive but to grow and significantly expand.

A number of notable additions to the faculty, and expansions of the University program, curricular and extra-curricular, were made under Dr. Talmage's comparatively brief tenure as president. Not all of them were solely the result of his ideas and impetus, of course, nor would he ever have thought of so claiming them. Many were extensions and implementations of concepts already projected. Others were the results of joint efforts with other members of the faculty. Some, indeed, were Dr. Talmage's own. But all were vigorously supported by the new president, and contributed to the development of the institution.

In the academic year 1894-95, the first of Dr. Talmage's administration, a Department of Philosophy was established, and courses in the general area of history and political science were brought together in an effective grouping which formed the foundation for establishing, the following year, a Department of History and Civics under Professor Joseph Whitely. In 1894, Dr. C. A. Whiting joined the faculty with the title of assistant professor of botany and zoology and the following year he was advanced to the rank of full professor and placed at the head of a Department of Natural History. A School of Mines, of obvious importance in a region of great mineral wealth, was established in 1896, under the terms of the 1894 Enabling Act, prelude to Utah's attaining statehood. The act provided 100,000 acres of land for support of a school of mines, a sort of "seed corn" concept for the development of one of the state's most important basic resources, mineral wealth.

In 1896 a Department of Economics and Sociology was set up under Professor George Coray, Dr. Talmage's fellow instructor and partner in the stereopticon enterprise at Brigham Young Academy more than a dozen years previously. Professor Coray also served as librarian and under his direction the University library expanded significantly in this period, a substantial aid being provided by President Talmage's strongly-worded plea to the 1897 Legislature.

Courses of evening lectures, open to the public as well as to students and faculty, were made a permanent part of the University program in 1895-96. President Talmage and Professors Whiting and G. M. Marshall acted as a special committee to plan and direct the program, and also participated as lecturers. Actually, there were two separate courses of lectures, one by members of the faculty and the other featuring non-campus personalities, leaders in a variety of fields, who were especially invited to appear. In the faculty series, the participants took subjects directly associated with their own instructional fields, but removed from the direct line of classroom teaching. President Talmage himself participated, in his capacity of professor of geology, being one of the group of teachers of scientific subjects who presented a subdivision of the over-all lecture course devoted to the general subject, "The Testimony of the Sciences in Favor of Theism." The presentations were rigidly non-sectarian, but definitely in keeping with the beliefs and attitudes of the vast majority of the community.

The *University of Utah Quarterly,* a campus publication devoted to academic, scientific, and literary matters, was proposed by the new president in his first year in office. The idea was endorsed by the faculty and approved by the Regents and the journal appeared as the official publication of the University through the academic years of 1895-96 and 1896-97.

Many distinguished members of the faculty came to the institution during Dr. Talmage's administration, or developed their programs as the institution turned its full efforts and energies toward the goal of attaining genuine university stature.

Among these were Joseph F. Merrill, who was to contribute so much in the area of chemistry and physics over a long span of years; Byron Cummings, Dr. Whiting, Professor Whitelock, and the young Richard R. Lyman who was instrumental in developing the School of Engineering. The Department of Modern Languages came into its own under Professor George R. Mathews, and Professor George M. Marshall organized and directed the University's first Department of English Language and Literature. The young Maude May Babcock, fresh from Eastern schools of drama and oratory, had joined the University faculty one year before Dr. Talmage, and was engaged in developing a program that brought distinction to the institution over a half-century of her energetic leadership.

Richard R. Lyman's connection with Dr. Talmage had its beginnings in 1894 when the former was president of the senior class at the University of Michigan. That distinguished institution had a program of lectures which deliberately sought to develop discussion in areas of controversy. As leader of a considerable colony of Utah students at the Ann Arbor institution, young Lyman had succeeded in having an invitation extended to Dr. Talmage to deliver a lecture on the subject "The Story of Mormonism."

The invitation had been extended before Dr. Talmage accepted the University of Utah presidency and temporarily disassociated himself from prominent Church-connected activities. However, he kept the Ann Arbor appointment with the approval of the University of Utah Board of Regents, as he would be appearing as an official representative neither of the University nor of the Church, but as a private individual.

The Michigan lecture series was nationally known both for its presentation of controversial issues and also for its rough treatment of guest lecturers, both while they occupied the podium and also afterward in the press. The Ann Arbor lecture community was no respecter of persons: Grover Cleveland, who appeared there between his two terms as President of the United States, had been treated most cavalierly.

Dr. Talmage found conditions fully up to advance notices when he arrived at Ann Arbor to fulfill his engagement. The town was profusely placarded with notices of the lecture on Mormonism, and the forthcoming lecture appeared to be a major subject for discussion in the community. The general atmosphere was one of lively anticipation of another unrestrained assault on the standard-bearer of an unpopular cause.

When James took the platform, the audience confirmed this impression. It was noisy and openly hostile.

Within a short time, however, the speaker wrought a transformation which astonished those present, particularly the University officials, who had never (by their own statement) seen anything like it in the course of the turbulent lecture series, and young Richard Lyman and the colony of Utah students who could scarcely believe the delightful evidence of their own eyes and ears. The lecture lasted an hour and a half, during which the audience showed no signs of restlessness, but (in James' words) "sighed, sometimes wept at the description of our people's sufferings and—think of it!—cheered most heartily at every success, even the mention of Brigham Young's defiance of Johnston's Army, sent by the President of the United States to chastise the Mormons."

Even the traditionally hostile press—hostile towards University of Michigan lecturers and even more hostile towards the Mormons—was favorable. A batch of newspaper clippings forwarded by Richard Lyman to Dr. Talmage at Ithaca, N.Y., where he delivered a similar lecture at Cornell University, displayed fairness and objectivity in their reporting and were "flattering" in their editorial comment.

The Cornell experience generally paralleled that at Ann Arbor. The "Utah Colony," headed by Ray Van Cott, received him warmly and the lecture itself was pronounced a great success, although perhaps less spectacularly so than that at Michigan. It was extensively applauded by a critical Cornell audience.

James' regular duties at the University of Utah included, of course, those of professor of geology as well as the administrative responsibilities of the presidency, and it is clear to see that the former were a joy to perform while the latter assumed more the role of a stern taskmaster. Field trips were a special delight to the scientist, and James confided almost guiltily that he felt "almost as a young boy on a holiday" whenever he could "get away from the turmoil of executive work and out into Nature's wilds."

During the summer of 1895 an extensive expedition into the wondrous and little-known desert country of Southeastern Utah was undertaken under the joint sponsorship of the University of Utah and the Deseret Museum. Funds provided by the Deseret Museum were what made the expedition possible in view of the extremely straitened financial circumstances of the state institution, and were another evidence of the tangible support which the LDS Church had promised the University. The expedition, which was in the field seven weeks, added significantly to the store of scientific knowledge of this sparsely-explored region, and brought quantities of valuable specimens to the growing University of Utah Museum and to the Deseret Museum. It also proved to be a rugged physical test for its participants and at times a hazardous adventure which narrowly missed tragedy.

President Talmage himself led the expedition, which on more than one occasion was reduced to a few swallows of water when out in remote high-cliff country where survival was literally a desperate race to reach one of the scarce and hard-to-find waterholes before the travelers' last drops of the life-sustaining fluid ran out.

The expedition's animals suffered as much or more than the men. Exhausted horses were exchanged for fresh beasts whenever possible at the scattered ranches along the way, and at one point the situation became so desperate that when bands of wild desert ponies were encountered, some were rounded up and pressed into service.

These were not the wild horses, legacy of the early Spanish explorers, which roam some remote areas of the West. They were branded animals turned out in the vast open country to feed as are range cattle; but they were "wild" in the sense of never having known saddle or harness, and "breaking" them to serve was a memorable task for the amateur cowboys.

Dr. Talmage noted that the action did not constitute "a case of horse stealing," as he was well acquainted with the officers of the company which owned the range animals, and that he would make suitable payment to them as soon as opportunity presented itself. The appropriation of range animals had to be carried out more than once, and Dr. Talmage recorded, somewhat tongue-in-cheek, that "we are becoming hardened in the practice of taking horses that do not belong to us." Fortunately a representative of the company which owned the animals was encountered on the way, and he promptly approved the emergency action that had been taken and made suitable arrangements for eventual settlement of the account.

The expedition achieved its purpose from a scientific point of view. There were no spectacular discoveries, but none had been expected. Aim of the undertaking had been to go into a little-known and -explored region and expand the meagre store of facts concerning its geography, geology, flora, and fauna which had been provided by the early explorers who had left some record of their findings. The long-range plan was to make this the first of a systematic series of expeditions that would cover the entire Southeastern Utah area and eventually the whole state. Unfortunately, various circumstances interfered with the immediate continuation of the planned program, and it was many years before it was resumed. The present-day Geological and Mineralogical Survey is fulfilling the concept in which that first University of Utah-Deseret Museum expedition was founded, but the first effort did add substantially to available knowledge of the least known and most scenically and geologically spectacular regions of the state—or of the world—including many photographs and a wagonload of specimens for the museums.

During the period when Dr. Talmage's working time was so filled with the administrative responsibilities of the University presidency and the professional interests of the geologist, a number of important events were recorded in his private life.

At Christmastime, 1894, with Sterling "going on" six years, little Paul reaching his third birthday, and a baby daughter Zella adding a feminine touch, James and May decided it was appropriate to decorate a family Christmas tree for the first time. It was a memorable occasion, with the tree's candlelight and reflections from the gaudy ornaments dancing in the eyes of the little ones, but the joyous smiles turned to heartbroken tears before the summer sun replaced the winter's snows. Zella became seriously ill in the late winter of 1894-95, and while intensive and loving care and frequent administration by the Priesthood kept her alive for many weeks and her parents retained hope of her complete recovery, she never did fully regain her health and strength. In early April, pneumonia attacked her tiny, weakened body, and early in the morning of April 27 she passed away. Parental grief

Sterling (upper left) and Paul, first of the Talmage children, in their early childhood. Below, May holds the baby Zella, only one of the eight children who did not grow to maturity.

was profound and lasting, though never fully released even in the privacy of personal journals.

There was great rejoicing some two years later when another child came to bless the Talmage home and it proved to be another girl, so especially desired after Zella's death. The new arrival, born August 16, 1896, was given the name Elsie, after her late maternal grandmother.

A number of scientific honors came to Dr. Talmage during his tenure as president of the University of Utah. In December, 1894, he received official word of his election as a Fellow of the Royal Society of Edinburgh, the problem of his non-British citizenship and the restriction in the Society's by-laws having been somehow resolved.

His reaction to the high honor was typical. He was deeply sensitive to the personal recognition, but preferred to regard it primarily as "a recognition of Utah and the 'Mormon' Church, in which I see the hand of God plainly manifest," adding reverently: "May the prestige thus bestowed be used in the service of God."

The effects of this event, in furthering the cause of the Church, were to reach over thousands of miles of space and more than three decades in time in ways that Dr. Talmage could scarcely have imagined at this time.

The *Deseret Evening News* of December 18 carried a highly laudatory (but somewhat inaccurate) article on the event and the following morning's *Herald* contained a brief, to-the-point paragraph:

> The *Herald* congratulates Dr. J. E. Talmage on receiving the distinguished honor of F.R.S. (Edin.), Fellow of the Royal Society of Edinburgh, a very exclusive title. But few Americans have ever been so favored, and that this has been conferred upon our fellow citizen is an honor to Utah as well as a deserved recognition of the pre-eminent abilities of one of her sons. Dr. Talmage will wear his new honors with becoming modesty and grace.

The event seems to have been completely ignored by the anti-Mormon *Tribune*.

Just a few days later James received word that he had been elected a Fellow of the Geological Society of London, having been proposed for membership by the curator of the London Museum of Practical Geology.

Soon thereafter, James learned of his election to the Tau Beta Pi Society of Lehigh University, an honorary organization of graduates of that institution who achieved unusual prominence in any field of professional endeavor.

During the term of Dr. Talmage's University presidency, a new item suddenly appears, and recurs with increasing frequency, in his routine journal entries: the bicycle. The new chain-driven machine had recently replaced the perilous high-wheeler and it achieved immediate popularity. James acquired one of the new machines, not as a hobby or physical conditioner but as a practical means of transportation. He used it not only to get about the city—an important consideration in a day when public transportation facilities were extremely limited—but also farther afield. James could, and did, take his "wheel" with him on the train to American Fork or Lake Point, from where he would ride to the Talmage farm on Provo Bench or up to Alpine to visit May's relatives, sometimes carrying Sterling on the handle bars. From this it is apparent that James was more than a dilettante cyclist, but his skill did not come easily. The story of the hard road of learning to master the mechanical steed appears nowhere in James' journal, but was a favorite family story, told by May with mischievous delight and by James with a touch of self-consciousness.

Some time after James had achieved reasonable proficiency in handling his machine on standard roads, he showed up at the front door one evening a full hour late for dinner and scarcely recognizable.

May nearly went into shock, for her husband was a frightening sight. Battered, bruised, and bleeding profusely, clothes torn in a dozen places and covered with dust and mud, James looked as though he had been caught in a riot, or at least a fight of unusual violence. Neither, it developed, had been the case.

Half a block from the Talmage home a single-plank footbridge crossed the ditch of running water that separated the street from the footpath. Until now, James had dismounted when he reached this point in a homeward journey, and crossed the narrow bridge on foot. Today, he had decided that he had reached the point in his development as a cyclist where he should no longer resort to this prudent maneuver, but rather ride over the bridge in the manner of an accomplished veteran of the two-wheeler.

Having so decided, James approached the bridge resolutely, confident that he would negotiate the tricky passage in a manner to be proud of and to impress neighbors, if any should chance to be watching, with his skill and casual daring. He turned sharply from the road toward the bridge with scarcely any diminution of speed. The result was spectacular and observers, if any there were, must indeed have been impressed, but in a very different way from that intended. The professor's bicycle went onto the plank at an oblique angle and quickly slid off the side, throwing its rider heavily into the ditchbank.

Dazed, bruised, bleeding, and humiliated, Dr. Talmage was not convinced that the difficult maneuver was beyond his skill. Rather, he was stubbornly determined to prove that he could and would master the difficulty.

For the next hour, the president of the University of Utah might have been observed trundling his bicycle fifty yards or so down the road from the bridge, mounting and riding furiously toward the plank crossing, turning onto it with grim-lipped determination—and plunging off it in a spectacular and bone-shaking crash into the rough ditchbank. Uncounted times this startling performance was repeated, but in the end mind triumphed over matter, will power over faltering reflexes, and the crossing was successfully made. Not just once, but enough times in succession to convince James that he was capable of performing the feat without mishap at any time he might desire to do so. From then on, he never again dismounted to cross the bridge, albeit he never made the crossing without experiencing deep-seated qualms which he kept carefully concealed from any who might be watching.

The episode had another interesting aftermath. A short time later, it was decided that May might participate in the pleasures and conveniences of cycling, it having become acceptable and even fashionable for ladies to ride the new bicycle. A ladies' model was duly purchased and May set out to learn to ride it, under James' tutelage. Acutely conscious of the difficulties involved, difficulties to test a rugged man and presumably much greater for a delicately-nurtured woman, James mapped a careful campaign of teaching on his part and learning on May's. He explained in his best professional manner the principles of physics involved, discussed the subtle "feel" of balancing the two-wheeled machine, and otherwise instructed his pupil in the intricate art she was setting out to learn.

For the first attempt at actual riding, the couple went to Liberty Park, where there was ample unobstructed room for a beginner to proceed with minimum hazards. May was seated on her new bicycle and James took firm hold of the seat post to give balance and steadiness and they started forward on the broad carriage drive that circumnavigated the park. As they went, May felt a pleasurable exhilaration. She accelerated her rate of pedalling until James was furiously trotting alongside and beginning to pant slightly. After a few hundred yards May decided she had had enough of the beginners' class, and thereupon graduated into the advanced course. She accelerated abruptly, pulling completely away from James' helpful grasp and rode on confidently alone. The surprised James struggled along in the wake of his rapidly-disappearing wife-cyclist, shouting out unheeded warnings and instructions with his labored breath. He made the full mile-and-one-half tour of the park on foot, hurrying lest May might have had an accident somewhere up ahead, until at last he found her serenely waiting at their point of departure, where his own bicycle had been left.

From that time on, cycling was a pleasant recreation which they frequently shared.

The years 1894-1897 were exciting and historic ones for the people of Utah, who witnessed the transition from territorial status to that of a sovereign state. This transformation was doubly sweet because of the many bitter disappointments that had come from earlier unsuccessful attempts to achieve statehood. After the long years of troubled relations with Federally-appointed governing officials, many of whom had been strongly anti-Mormon, the boon of self-government which came with statehood was one to be cherished indeed.

Dr. Talmage had been directly involved in the transformation in his capacity of President of the University of Utah, though only to a limited degree. He had conferred with the educational committee of the Constitutional Convention and had addressed the convention proper on the educational needs of Utah, and he had worked closely with the final territorial and first state Legislatures on University matters.

The 1897 Legislature took action regarding the institution that had a direct and profound effect on Dr. Talmage's personal plans and professional career. While the worst of the effects of the financial panic had passed and the economy was recovering, the infant state was far from affluent, and in an economy move the 1897 Legislature put a ceiling on salaries that could be paid at the institution. The General Appropriations Bill gave $73,000 to the University for the ensuing biennium, but appended the following rider:

> "*Provided:* that no officer or member of the faculty of said University, for all service rendered to the state during the term herein named [two academic years ending June 30, 1899] shall be paid any salary in excess of $2,500 per annum."

The restriction in itself might not have been too disturbing to Dr. Talmage, if the financial condition of the state had made it necessary. He had many times shown his willingness to serve for limited remuneration in times of difficulty. When emergency circumstances had required the imposition of a 15 per cent salary cut on the University faculty in late 1893, when he was a part-time member of that body, he had accepted it willingly and had criticized the few faculty members who had openly complained about a move that was necessary to keep the institution in operation.

The 1897 action, however, had a different aspect. Dr. Talmage was serving in a dual capacity, as president of the University and as Deseret Professor of Geology. The teaching position was an endowed chair with a guaranteed salary of $2,400 a year. The legislative restriction would mean that Dr. Talmage would have to perform all the administrative duties of the presidency, and suffer through all of the attendant headaches and problems, for a total of $100 per year. James understandably felt that this was an unreasonable demand, and that in failing to make provision for the special circumstances, the Legislature had placed him in an untenable position. His heart was far more in the activities of teaching and scientific research than in those of administration, and he could honestly feel that he had successfully performed the most important tasks for which he had originally been asked to assume the presidency of the institution: the pulling together of a strife-torn faculty and setting the university on a new course of progress.

After a period of mature and sometimes painful reflection and analysis, he determined to resign the presidency but retain the chair of geology.

While it is certain that the action of the Legislature was the basic reason for Dr. Talmage's resignation, it is also true that there had been some dissent on the campus and some faculty members had been notified that their contracts would not be renewed the following year. This action had been fully supported by the Board of Regents, to whom the complete background story had been made known, though it had not been made public. Nevertheless, there were widespread and unfounded rumors that Dr. Talmage had been requested to resign, a situation deeply disturbing to Dr. Talmage himself.

The *Deseret Evening News* of April 5, 1897, in reporting the resignation, commented that it "was not entirely unexpected, as it has been known for some time that all was not working as harmoniously as might be desired at the state's leading educational institution." Other sectors of the press openly hinted at the rumors of a forced resignation.

The Regents, to whom all the facts were known, confirmed Dr. Talmage's retention as professor of geology.

At the end of the academic year 1896-97 Dr. Talmage asked for and was granted a special meeting of the executive committee of the Board of Regents, at which he made a final report on the contingency fund placed at the disposal of the president of the University, the report being duly audited and accepted. The presidency passed to Dr. Joseph T. Kingsbury, who had been instrumental in getting Dr. Talmage to accept the position three years previously and who had served as vice president during Dr. Talmage's term as president.

At the same meeting of the executive council, Dr. Talmage requested and received a leave of absence to attend the International Geological Congress to be held in Russia, before returning to his duties as Deseret Professor of Geology.

# A Succession of European Visits

The trip to Russia in 1897 was a memorable one for James E. Talmage, and later for all the members of his family, who could never forget the all-too-rare evenings when "Father" told fascinating stories of the exotic sights and sounds, food and drink, customs and ceremonies in the land of the Czars. Dr. Talmage was a true traveller with a touch of Marco Polo in his makeup, no mere tourist who visited foreign lands in order to say that he had "been there." His journals contain hundreds of pages of detail concerning his travels.

In the journals, famous sights and places are touched upon, sometimes in detail when James was deeply stirred, but mostly with comparatively brief mention and a terse notation, "see guide book." His own detailed observations are usually more concerned with the geology, flora and fauna of foreign lands (though most such references are relatively brief, ending in repeated directions to "see field notes," in which James recorded scientific observations in meticulous detail) ; the dress, eating habits, attitudes, and general way of life of the peoples amongst whom he moved. The journal pages covering the trip to Russia contain sketches of unusual ways of harnessing draft animals, of strange manners of constructing transmission lines, of the high porcelain stoves—complete even to diagrams of the flow of the draft airs to keep the fires burning—and even the unique design of the hats worn by Russian droskshi drivers.

The experience of the 1897 International Geological Congress offered wide scope for indulging James' delight in travel and learning, and he made the most of it. He became officially a delegate representing the Royal Society of Edinburgh, and he not only attended the formal sessions of the Congress in St. Petersburg in late August and early September, but prior to that also participated in a trip into interior Russia, which was offered to delegates at their choice, crossing the Urals into Asian Siberia as far as Niji Novgorod. James went from London to St. Petersburg, point of departure and return for the excursion to the Urals, via Denmark, Sweden, and Finland, travelling by boat with frequent stopovers ashore during which James obtained close-up views of the Scandinavian countries and customs.

In Russia, the Congress delegates were officially guests of the Czar, although most of them did not meet the Russian ruler in person.

Dr. Talmage returned to Europe again the following year, visiting the western Norwegian fjords as far north as Trondhjem. When he returned to Britain following the Scandinavian excursion, he engaged in a whirlwind lecture tour that became a legend in the British Mission.

One of the greatest obstacles which the missionaries were encountering was the widespread and stubborn prejudice of the British people against The Church of Jesus Christ of Latter-day Saints, based on the lurid falsehoods regarding their moral practices that were circulated and believed at every level of society. Mission authorities and missionaries in the field were at their wits' end trying to devise ways to penetrate the wall of prejudice and get through to the people some basic truths about the way of life in Utah and among its Mormon inhabitants.

According to an editorial in the *Millennial Star* of August 11, 1898, a suggestion was made that a series of lectures, illustrated with stereopticon views of Utah and its people, be presented in key cities throughout Britain. This plan was approved at a meeting of the British Mission presidency and conference (district) presidents in Birmingham in January, 1898, and later given official approval by the First Presidency of the Church.

Key to the success of the venture was to have a lecturer whose credentials would be instantly recognized and respected by the British public. Dr. Talmage's name immediately came to mind. He was an experienced and effective lecturer and, more important, he was a member of a number of high-level British scientific societies, which gave him the required stature in the eyes of British press and public. When it was learned that Dr. Talmage was to be in Europe in the summer of 1898, the lecture series was scheduled to fit the dates of his visit.

The midsummer timing of the lectures appeared to be unfortunate, but it was unavoidable as Dr. Talmage's position on the University of Utah faculty prevented his journeying to Europe except during the summer quarter when regular classwork was suspended. The *Millennial Star* noted that proprietors of lecture halls that were engaged throughout the land warned that "it was the wrong time of year for a stereopticon lecture: darkness did not ensue until 9:15 P.M. The weather was too hot, and above all it was August Bank Holiday Week, wherein there is a general migration from town to country and the seaside on the part of everyone who can afford it; why, even the theaters were closed. If it were only in the wintertime, season of long evenings, the result would be so different."

In spite of these ominous warnings, Mission authorities went ahead with their plans.

When Dr. Talmage landed in Newcastle-on-Tyne on his return from Norway, he found the city liberally sprinkled with "flaming posters and handbills" announcing a lecture that same evening, and a schedule of appearances in eight other English cities, as well as in Glasgow, Scotland, and Belfast, Ireland. This was a somewhat more extensive program than James had anticipated and the schedule was extremely tight, calling for a lecture per evening with no rest breaks except between the final two appearances in Belfast on August 3 and Wigan, near Liverpool, on August 5.

Dr. Talmage had been informed of the warning that "audiences could not be brought together for lectures at this season," but the Newcastle experience was a heartening refutation of the pessimistic predictions. The audience "was all that could be desired, both as to size and also, and particularly, as to quality. The people gave their attention and showed marked sympathy with the subject, applauding the descriptions of Mormon perseverance under suffering, and cheering the mention of the great leader, Brigham Young."

After the lecture Dr. Talmage and Elder Robert Anderson of Logan, who had been assigned the task of operating the stereopticon, took the midnight train for Norwich, where the following night's lecture was scheduled. This was a pattern that was to become all too familiar in the next few tightly-packed days.

The reception in Newcastle was repeated in Norwich, where a full-house audience of 800 was deeply and favorably impressed. The same reception was met all along the way and can perhaps be best indicated by the written reports of the missionaries laboring in the cities where the lectures were presented, and especially by the reports published in the local press. These, particularly the press reports, would not be tinged with any subjectivity which might unconsciously attach to Dr. Talmage's own reactions, and any prejudice which might exist would definitely be hostile rather than friendly in the case of British newspapers, which had frequently been bitter and even vituperative in their denunciations of the Mormons.

Typical reaction was shown by the *Independent* of Barnsley, a Sheffield suburb, which printed a lengthy account of Dr. Talmage's August 1 lecture, from which the following is excerpted:

> There was an exceptionally good attendance and . . . the lecture, illustrated by limelight views, was highly appreciated. . . . Descriptions, eloquent and graphic, were given, illustrative of the [Mormon pioneers'] wearisome march across the desert fraught with danger at every step; the first efforts at raising crops in the desert; the devastation of the fields by the dreaded Rocky Mountain locusts, the seasonal arrival of the sea gulls and the providential destruction of the insect pests; . . . the drafting of the "Mormon Battalion" to serve in the war between the United States and Mexico; and the more recent and rapid development of the new State.

The *Bradford Observer* noted that Dr. Talmage, "Professor of Geology at the University in Salt Lake City and a Fellow of the Royal Society of Edinburgh," was "making a lecture tour of Great Britain, giving addresses in all the principal towns" and commented:

> Possessed of a good platform manner, he is enabled to enlist the attention and sympathies of his audiences to a marked degree, and on Saturday evening [July 30] his remarks were followed with close attention by a large audience.

The *Glasgow Evening Times* stated in part:

> The doctor is worth hearing . . . so interesting was his manner and so fascinating his style that he held the attention of his audience for close on a couple of hours. . . . He did not preach Mormonism, but he praised the Mormons in many an eloquent sentence. . . . We were shown temples and colleges and cooperative buildings —marvellously fine structures which stand as monuments of Mormon industry and culture. . . .

British Mission authorities were overjoyed with the results of the lecture series, which surpassed anticipatory hopes. The *Millennial Star* editorial discussion of August 11 recorded, almost in awe:

> Never in the history of the Church have such a high class array of well-known halls been thrown open for the use of the Latter-day Saints. In almost every case the best hall that money could furnish in every town has been secured. In Oldham [a suburb of Manchester] it is estimated that 700 people were reluctantly turned away from the doors [after the hall was filled to its capacity of nearly 1600]. It remained for the year 1898 to produce the phenomenal spectacle of men rising to their feet and cheering the mention of Brigham Young's name. . . .

The lecture tour produced some most peculiar situations. In Wigan, near Liverpool, all seats were filled and scores were occupying standing room in the hall an hour before time for the lecture, in spite of a rainstorm of almost torrential proportions. For this remarkable turnout, at least an "assist" came from one Heeps—a bitter enemy of the Church and a constant thorn in the side of its missionary representatives in Wigan—who had tirelessly canvassed the town to advertise the lecture, even going so far as to distribute handbills which he had printed at his own expense. It developed that the man had read the advertising placards and had presumed that the speaker was to be T. DeWitt Talmage, the Brooklyn firebrand evangelist, whose violently anti-Latter-day Saint pamphlet "Mormonism—an Exposure" was well known in Britain.

With a substantial part of the audience consisting of Heeps' Mormon-baiters, the atmosphere at the beginning of the lecture had a perceptible tinge of hostility, but within a short time the listeners were on the side of the lecturer and soon were cheering the saints' triumphs and groaning in their tribulations, as had audiences elsewhere along the lecture trail. Following the lecture, Mr. Heeps wailed loudly that he had been fraudulently induced to spend almost "a quid" (£ 1/0/0) of his own money to advertise an exposé of the Mormons, only to hear that despised people extolled; but he found few sympathizers.

Although the lecture tour appeared to be a decided success at every point along the way, the high point was undoubtedly reached in Glasgow, Scotland.

Young David O. McKay, who had been a student of Dr. Talmage at the University of Utah prior to coming on his mission, was president of the Scottish Conference (District) and he had pulled out all stops in making arrangements for the Glasgow appearance. He had engaged the City Hall for the lecture, and obtained the consent of the United States consul, Samuel H. Taylor, to serve as chairman of the meeting and that of a distinguished Scottish musician, Professor Harold Ryder, to furnish organ music. The lecture was a full dress affair for the occupants of reserved seats, for which a double charge was made. Skeptics shook their heads and said President McKay had overreached himself and that the meeting would be a miserable failure.

Indeed, disaster very nearly did strike, but from an entirely unsuspected quarter.

The Glasgow lecture immediately followed the Barnsley appearance, requiring a train journey of some 250 miles. Travel arrangements were left entirely to the mission authorities, as Dr. Talmage and Elder Anderson had their hands full with other matters, and when they were escorted to the railway station in Sheffield at 7.20 on the morning of August 2 to board the 7:30 express for Glasgow they assumed that everything was in order. To their consternation, they discovered that a mistake had been made. The Glasgow express had departed at 7 o'clock, on schedule, and the next train for that destination did not leave for a considerable time; it was late in starting, and as it travelled it fell further and further behind schedule.

Elder McKay had especially requested Dr. Talmage to arrive early in order to meet a number of distinguished guests before the start of the lecture. As the day wore on, it became more and more clearly evident that not only would he fail to arrive "early," but would be definitely late, and there was growing concern lest the arrival in Glasgow would be so late as to rule out all possibility of a lecture appearance. Elder McKay had been apprised of the situation by telegram sent by the mission authorities, and there was nothing to do but wait and hope.

As evening arrived, the skies blackened and a crashing thunderstorm suddenly broke, rain falling in torrents. This added a stage-effects setting to the travellers' anxiety, but also provided an unorthodox solution to at least a part of the problem.

As has been noted, the lecture was to be a formal affair, requiring Dr. Talmage to appear in white tie and tails. At the time scheduled for his appearance at the hall, the lecturer had more the appearance of a stoker, the soot and grime of a dozen hours' travel in the loose-windowed trains of 1898 having deposited the inevitable layers of soot and cinder on the travellers. Elder McKay had reserved a hotel room in which Dr. Talmage was supposed to clean up and change clothing, but obviously there would be no time to use it. The time had come to take desperation measures, and the driving rain outside offered novel means of doing so.

Dr. Talmage and Elder Anderson had a compartment to themselves and the train was one in which the compartments extended the full width of the train, with no communicating corridor, insuring that their privacy would not be disturbed. Dr. Talmage stripped to the waist, and opened a window. Then Elder Anderson grasped him firmly about the knees, for all the world as though making a football tackle from behind, and held on resolutely as the professor projected his upper body out the window into the rain, turning and twisting so that the pelting rain struck him from every direction. After thirty or forty seconds of this, Elder Anderson would haul him, coughing and sputtering, back into the train compartment, where pocket handkerchiefs and Dr. Talmage's about-to-be-discarded shirt were used to "towel" him down and remove a layer of accumulated grime. The maneuver was repeated at least a dozen times, and must have presented a startling sight if any wayside travellers chanced to catch a glimpse of it. If any there were, they doubtless told lurid tales of a desperate suicide attempt, with the would-be self-destructor being hauled back within the speeding train by an unseen rescuer.

In the end the treatment was adjudged sufficiently effective to permit the lecturer to don his gleaming white shirt and tie and "full dress suit." When the train reached Glasgow Dr. Talmage emerged from the sooty compartment looking every inch the suave and polished platform performer.

A carriage was waiting at the station and there followed a fast gallop through the city, first to the Argyle Hotel to pick up Mr. Taylor, the Consul, and thence to the City Hall where an audience of more than 1500 had been patiently sitting for more than an hour.

"I am sure the audience could have been excused had there been impatient manifestations," Dr. Talmage wrote, "but no speaker could ask for a more attentive and sympathetic group of listeners." The *Glasgow Evening Times,* as quoted above, recorded that the assembly sat in close attention for "close on a couple of hours" longer after the lecture began.

David O. McKay wrote in the *Millennial Star:*

> For two hours and five minutes the lecturer held [the audience] spellbound, only interrupted here and there by a great round of applause, and when he mentioned closing they urged him to continue. . . . The good effects of the lecture are already realized. Businessmen are eager to tell anyone interested in the meeting about the merits of Dr. Talmage as a lecturer. They treat us as courteously as they can. . . . The next time Dr. Talmage appears in Glasgow he can fill the City Hall with half the amount of advertising.

The *Millennial Star*, speaking "on behalf of the Presidency of the European Mission and the Elders laboring in Great Britain," took occasion to "heartily thank Dr. Talmage for the splendid series of lectures he has delivered, which have been the means of removing a vast amount of prejudice, that could only otherwise have been accomplished by a personal trip to the State of Utah [by each of those who attended the lectures]."

As soon as possible after completing the lecture series, Dr. Talmage turned his face toward home, sailing August 6 on the Cunard steamer *Campania*. He reached Salt Lake on August 19 and a week later dispatches relating the story of the successful lecture tour, mailed by British Mission authorities, appeared in the *Deseret Evening News* (August 26, 1898), including extensive quotations from the British press and with laudatory editorial comment added.

James went to Europe again in the summer of 1899 to attend meetings of the scientific societies of which he was a fellow, and of the Victorian Institute (also known as the Philosophical Society of Britain) to which he had been elected earlier in the year. This was an organization "professing as its chief purpose the study of the harmonies between science and the revealed word of God" in which Dr. Talmage had been proferred membership for some time. He had finally accepted on the advice of the General Authorities of the Church.

It was at the Authorities' urging, also, that Dr. Talmage undertook the 1899 European journey. Much as he desired to attend the meetings and renew his many friendships with leading British men of science, James felt the increasing weight of domestic responsibilities—there were four living children now, James Karl having been born on August 29, 1898—and both the considerable cost of another European journey and his reluctance to leave May to manage the children through the summer vacation without his assistance weighed against the venture.

However, when President Lorenzo Snow proposed that the Church pay $300 toward the cost of the trip, James felt that he should accede to the wishes of the Church Authorities. He declined the offer of financial assistance and viewed the journey as a missionary labor, noting in his journal:

> Knowing as I do how embarrassed the Authorities are in a financial sense, and realizing that it is the duty of every member of the Church rather to aid the authorities in ridding the Church of debt than increase the burden . . . I volunteered to go at my own expense. Heavy as is the burden of cost, it is not greater than that borne by the missionaries, who leave their occupations and lose all chance of securing income during their two or three years' absence. While I have no money to spare, I am thankful to be able to undertake the journey with little danger of running into debt thereby.

The 1899 trip was confined to its essential purpose of attending meetings of the Royal Society of Edinburgh, the Geological and Microscopical Societies, and the Victorian Institute, and conducting discussions with British men of science, particularly James' close friends in Scotland.

Returning home in mid-August, James felt that it might be a considerable time before he should be able to return again to the land of his birth. Although he could not know this at the time, it was to be a full quarter-century before he again saw Europe, and then he would go to preside over the British and European Missions and would be able to take with him Maia and members of their family.

# CHAPTER SIXTEEN

# "The Articles of Faith"

The *Deseret Evening News* of March 10, 1899, carried the following notice at the head of its editorial column:

## Official Announcement

During the early part of April there will be issued by the *Deseret News* a Church work entitled "The Articles of Faith," the same being a series of lectures on the principal doctrines of The Church of Jesus Christ of Latter-day Saints, by Dr. James E. Talmage. The lectures were prepared by appointment of the First Presidency, and the book will be published by the Church. It is intended for use as a text book in the Church schools, Sunday schools, [Mutual] Improvement Associations, quorums of the Priesthood, and other Church organizations in which the study of Theology is pursued, and also for individual use among the members of the Church. The work has been approved by the First Presidency, and I heartily commend it to the members of the Church.

(President) *Lorenzo Snow.*

This was the first public announcement of the publication of a bound volume, but the project had long been known to many Church members, and the eventual appearance of such a book had been eagerly awaited. The lectures referred to by President Snow were those which had been discontinued when Dr. Talmage was being considered for the presidency of the

University of Utah, and a number of them had already appeared in print in the *Juvenile Instructor*.

The seed of the idea from which the book was born was apparently first planted on September 14, 1891. On that day, Dr. Talmage met with President Wilford Woodruff and his counselors and thereafter noted in his journal:

> It is the intention of the brethren to cause to be published a class work in Theology for use in the Church schools and Religion classes generally. The need for such a work has long been felt among the teachers of the Latter-day Saints. . . . Several preliminaries have to be arranged before the work is begun; but the First Presidency have expressed to me their intention of appointing me to do the labor. I find myself very busy already, but I have never yet found it necessary to decline any labor appointed to me by the Holy Priesthood; and in the performance of duties so entailed, as my day, so has my strength ever been.

Various delays intervened and it was the last day of January, 1893, before the First Presidency directed Dr. Talmage to proceed with the work under discussion. An oral charge to do so was later confirmed in writing, a communication dated February 20, 1893, and signed by President Woodruff and President Joseph F. Smith, President George Q. Cannon being out of the city at the time. The letter reiterated the need for "properly analyzed text and reference books in the theological and religious subjects, for use in our Church schools, Sunday schools, etc.," and went on to give a specific charge:

> It is our desire that a book suitable for the purposes named should be placed in the hands of our people as soon as possible. Knowing your experience in this direction, we should be pleased to have you prepare such a work.

In October of the same year, the General Authorities decided to act on Dr. Talmage's suggestion to establish a special theological class in connection with the LDS College. The class would meet each Sunday with Dr. Talmage as its instructor, and the course of study would be the material to be incorporated in the textbook which he had been commissioned to prepare.

The first session of the theological class was held on
Sunday, October 29, 1893, meeting in the lecture room in the
new building intended for use of the proposed Church university. This room was filled to capacity and beyond. Chairs
were brought in from the adjoining college building and
placed in the aisles, on the speaker's platform, any place and
every place that they could be crowded in. James noted that
when he had proposed the weekly theological class he had
not dreamed of anything on this scale. He had in mind "a
small body of students, with perhaps a few outsiders." He
wrote:

> . . . but the Presidency of the Church directed that the scope
> of the class be enlarged. Had not the course which made so large a
> class possible originated with the authorities of the Priesthood, I
> should mistrust the outlook. Things great, substantial, and lasting
> usually have very small beginnings. Our class has a very large
> inception. . . . So many applicants had to be denied admission that
> it was decided . . . to meet next Sunday in the Assembly Hall.

If the class teacher was disturbed by the large turnout
at that first session, subsequent classes in the Assembly Hall
could have done nothing to reassure him. The first session
in the larger quarters brought an attendance between 500
and 600, and the figure rose to "not less than 900" on the
following Sunday. From there it continued to move upward,
past the 1,000 mark, thence to 1,100, to 1,200, and by April,
1894, was pushing close to the 1,300 figure.

In November, 1893, the First Presidency directed that
the lecture material be published in full, in serial form, in the
*Juvenile Instructor*. In view of the fact that the material was
to be made of permanent record as it was delivered, the
author requested the First Presidency to appoint a "committee on criticism" to pass on it before publication. Such a
committee was appointed and comprised Elders Francis M.
Lyman (chairman) and Abraham H. Cannon of the Council
of the Twelve; President George Reynolds of the First Council

of Seventy; Elder John Nicholson; and Dr. Karl G. Maeser. The committee worked closely with the author, and on occasion referred questions to still higher authority, frequently going to the First Presidency. Once Dr. Talmage was called from the Salt Lake Temple, where he had gone with May to do ordinance work, for a meeting with the committee and the First Presidency to discuss certain doctrinal points, the discussion lasting several hours. The doctrinal questions were further discussed later in the day in a meeting of the First Presidency and Council of the Twelve, following which James "was told by one of the Apostles on the Committee that I was authorized to proclaim this as doctrine in the theology class."

On April 1, 1894, attendance at the weekly class was probably the largest it had ever been, and it came as a stunning surprise to those assembled when Dr. Talmage, after finishing the day's lesson and answering as many questions from class members as time permitted, announced that this would be the final meeting of the group for the foreseeable future as the class was being discontinued.

Elder Abraham H. Cannon of the Council of the Twelve, a member of the "committee on criticism" of the class lecture material, at this point took over for the teacher and read to the class a letter from the First Presidency to Dr. Talmage, advising discontinuance of the weekly meetings and giving reasons for such action.

Chief among them, of course, was that the emissaries from the University of Utah had come to the First Presidency to urge that Dr. Talmage take the presidency of that institution. In these circumstances, it was felt that it would be inconsistent for Dr. Talmage to occupy a prominent position in the teaching of Church theology while directing the affairs of a non-sectarian institution. James clearly saw the logic of the position taken by the First Presidency and agreed with it. Yet he felt real reluctance to abandon, even temporarily, an undertaking to which he was deeply committed in his innermost feelings.

"I feel much regret at seeing the class come to a close," he wrote on the Sunday evening following the final session.

"For the seed of success that has come to the class, I reverentially acknowledge the Hand of God. May the seed so planted yet produce healthful growth and pleasing fruit."

The plans for the "class work on Theology" lay dormant until 1898, when the First Presidency requested Dr. Talmage to resume work on its preparation. He had resigned the University presidency the previous year, and the reasons which had shaped the decision to interrupt the work no longer applied. Dr. Talmage remained a member of the teaching faculty of the University, but this did not impose the same restrictions as he had been under as chief administrative officer of the institution.

The First Presidency requested that the resumed work be pressed to completion "with all reasonable speed," and James did his best to comply.

The committee on criticism was revived with its original membership, except for Elder Cannon, who had passed away and whose place was taken by Elder Anthon H. Lund, also of the Council of the Twelve. Final reading of the manuscript to the committee was completed on January 5, 1899, although there were some further discussions directly with the First Presidency. James was astonished by the suggestion of the Presidency that the book be published, not by the author as an individual, but by the Church. This was done, though James wrote in his journal that while he was deeply appreciative of the honor, "I hardly felt to urge the matter, for I don't think the Church is rightly to be made responsible for slips and errors that will inevitably appear in the book."

The printing job was given to the Deseret News Press, and new type was ordered from the East especially for it. The first "form" (16-page) proof was placed in the author's hands on February 25, 1899, and a promise of "a form a day" (Sundays excepted, of course) was fulfilled, so that the final proof was read on April 1, and the objective was met of having the book available for April Conference visitors.

In 1923, a major revision (relating mostly to style, although including some changes in text) was undertaken, and on March 14, 1924—just a quarter-century after the original notice of publication—the *Deseret News* again carried an official announcement by the First Presidency of the impending publication of the book *The Articles of Faith,* this time in the twelfth (revised) edition. The edition sold out so rapidly that the appearance of the thirteenth edition was announced in a *Deseret News* editorial just a few weeks later, on April 25, 1924.

The book has gone through 50 editions (including 283,000 copies)[1] in English, and has been translated into many foreign languages. It is still widely used as a textbook in Church classes seventy years after it was written and almost forty years after its author's death.

---

[1]Much of the material in this chapter appeared in an article in the *Instructor* of November, 1965. At that time it was noted that 42 editions, including 243,000 copies, of *The Articles of Faith* had been printed. In the ensuing five years, eight more editions totalling 40,000 additional copies, were printed.

CHAPTER
SEVENTEEN

# The Professional Period

Following his resignation from the presidency of the University of Utah in 1897 and the last of the annual European excursions in 1899, James E. Talmage entered on a new era in his life which may be termed the professional period. He devoted an increasing proportion of his time to private consultation in the field of geology, particularly mining geology, one for which his years of study and research and rugged field work had particularly fitted him.

The professional era did not come abruptly with a conscious decision to turn to this way of life and a corresponding abandonment of other responsibilities, but rather it developed over a period of time, at first slowly and then with accelerating emphasis. This was an era of furious diversified mining activity in Utah and the Mountain West, when the exploitation of the area's abundant mineral resources was in full swing. The Valley of the Great Salt Lake claimed the title of "smelter capital of the world." Many active districts such as Park City, Tintic, Milford, Marysvale, and Alta were vying with one another in production from established mines and the development of new ones. Production companies were constantly engaged in exploratory and development operations, looking to the future. Many individuals and newly-formed companies were eager to get into the sometimes lucrative, often heartbreaking business of mining. They sought not only the precious metals, gold and silver, but also copper, lead, zinc and such minerals as antimony and manganese, for which the nation's expanding industrial economy was making increasing demand. Some interest was developing in non-metallic minerals with commercial value.

Services of competent geologists capable of evaluating mineral claims and deposits were in demand, and the demand continued to grow. As mining claims and operations multiplied, so did legal conflicts and the services of private consultants to develop accurate field data and competently present them in court were increasingly sought. As a consultant's reputation grew, so did the demand for his services and the fees which he could command. Dr. Talmage soon became known as one of the most valued and highest paid consulting geologists in the West.

Remuneration of expert consultants was not large in comparison to the fortunes made by the relatively few mining operators and speculators who struck it rich, but it was more than merely respectable in the economic scale of the day. For the first and only time in his life, James E. Talmage found himself commanding an income well above the decent subsistence level and enjoying a modest degree of affluence. He did not become wealthy, by any stretch of imagination, but he was able to provide more of the comforts of life for his growing family and to put a modest amount aside for the future—an important consideration as it developed, for in a very few years he was to be called to devote full time to the Church and for the rest of his life would receive minimal financial remuneration.

On numerous occasions in the past, Dr. Talmage had been retained as a consultant for specific short-term assignments in the fields of geology, chemistry, or metallurgy, but the beginning of the professional consultant phase of his career appears to have come in May, 1900, when he was called into a case involving irrigation rights, another subject of vital and growing interest in the expanding semi-arid West. It was also one which was frequently intertwined with mining problems, when mine tunnels became major conduits for underground water.

After this initial professional engagement others followed, at first occasionally, then with increasing frequency, until virtually every moment of James' free time was occupied in this pursuit. And "free time" may be a questionable term to de-

Dr. Talmage was an accomplished horseman, but usually preferred somewhat less rough country to ride in. His examinations of mining properties took him into the most rugged terrain. Over smoother ground, he often "galloped furiously" between locations where he had appointments, in order to keep up with tight schedules.

Dr. Talmage looks more like a hard rock miner than a highly respected consulting geologist as he pauses for a brief after-dinner rest on the porch of a boarding house at a mine. It may take a keen eye to identify the geologist, in his rough outdoor clothing and circular cap.

Looking anything but an ivory tower scholar, James E. Talmage emerges from an underground mine which he had been inspecting in his professional capacity as a geologist.

scribe the hours squeezed out between Professor Talmage's campus responsibilities and his Church duties which were increasing rather than diminishing over this time. He was named to the General Board of the Deseret Sunday School Union in October, 1901, and thereafter filled regular stake conference assignments in that capacity, and on a number of occasions he was called by the First Presidency to make cross-country journeys to fill special speaking assignments.

On many occasions, professional and Church duties were fitted into the same tightly-scheduled trip. James might make as many as half-a-dozen preliminary field examinations over a period of two to four days, "galloping furiously" on horseback over rough canyon roads between properties to be examined and riding no less furiously to reach some nearby town in the evening to fill a lecture engagement under the auspices of the Mutual Improvement Associations or in aid of a ward or stake building fund. Sometimes such lectures were scheduled without the speaker being aware of the fact, when local stake or ward authorities learned that Dr. Talmage was to be in their vicinity. Almost every weekend through this period, James' journal contains a terse entry noting that he took the Saturday night train home (rarely did such trains have sleeping cars) and not infrequently he arrived with just time to bathe, shave, change clothes and hurry to the first of the Church assignments that filled his Sabbath. Usually he would board an early train Monday to return to the scene of the field work in which he was engaged. Field work of course was frequently associated with appearances in the law courts to testify as an "expert witness," sometimes over a period of many days.

At first James fitted what consulting assignments he could around his teaching schedule, and crowded them into every holiday and vacation period. As the demand for his professional services increased and the pressures became almost intolerably heavy, he considered resigning his professorship at the University of Utah to devote more time to his consulting practice. In September, 1903, James consulted the First Presidency—in their capacity of "assigns of the Salt Lake Literary and Scientific Society who had the nominating power for the

Deseret Professorship of Geology"—about his resignation from that post, or at least being granted a leave of absence for a year or more. James was requested to retain the post "for the present," but submitted a formal letter of resignation, to be held in abeyance until the time should be judged ripe for its acceptance and publication.

In 1907 when James learned that he was about to be renominated for another extended term in the faculty post, he urgently requested that his resignation be accepted and announced, and this time his wishes were acceded to. On July 8, news of his resignation was published in the press. He had occupied the chair of geology at the University for thirteen years, including the three years during which he had also served as president of the institution.

One of Dr. Talmage's last official acts as professor of geology was to fulfill a long-held ambition and direct the installation of a seismograph on the University of Utah campus. The installation was completed June 29, 1907, and extensively discussed in all of the Salt Lake City newspapers. The earthquake-detecting instrument was the first to be set up in the Mountain West and was one of a comparatively few in the nation and the world at that time. The newspaper accounts were extensive and included numerous pictures of the strange apparatus, and it was noted that the first public demonstration proceeded "without a hitch or a hint of a hitch occurring in operation." Reporters and their readers were particularly impressed that the instrument could detect movements in the crust of the earth occurring halfway around the world ("Earthquakes Anywhere in the World Can Now Sign Their Own Names," proclaimed a sub-headline in the *Deseret Evening News*) yet could be affected by so delicate a pressure as a person's breathing.

Freed of his teaching obligation, James felt a relief from driving pressure that he had rarely known in his busy life, although his remaining schedule of professional activities and Church duties was certainly heavy by any standards.

When the Semi-Annual Conference of the Church convened in October, 1907, James noted with deep satisfaction that for the first time in more than a dozen years he was free to attend most of the meetings. He was able to spend many legal holidays at home, or on family outings, a rare and cherished privilege not only for himself but also for Maia and the children.

After leaving the University, Dr. Talmage opened a private office in the Sharon Building, on the east corner of Richards Street at South Temple. Three years later he moved west across Richards Street into the Vermont Building (now Beneficial Life Building) when the Deseret Museum was located there after having its exhibits packed away in storage for several years. Museum exhibits had been packed away when the previous quarters had been turned over to the University as part of the endowment of the Deseret Chair of Geology.

Dr. Talmage's consulting practice expanded rapidly as more time was made available for it, and he was called to make field examinations in all of the major mining districts in Utah and frequently travelled to Idaho, Montana, eastern Nevada, and even to Oregon. Much of the time field work was followed by appearances in court, and some celebrated cases stretched out over periods of years.

One case of unusual interest and which is illustrative of Dr. Talmage's work as a consultant, involved the question of alleged damage to agricultural crops caused by fumes emitted by the smelters in Salt Lake Valley—an issue familiar to residents of the area more than half a century later. The case led Dr. Talmage into experiences that were both physically and psychologically harrowing, and which were about as far removed from the traditional "ivory tower" realm of the college professor as could be imagined.

In order to analyze the content of the smelter smoke at full strength, Dr. Talmage and his assistant, William Blum, climbed the maintenance ladders to the top of the United States Smelting Company's 250-foot smokestack at West Jordan and the Highland Boy stack in Bingham, spending several hours on the catwalks atop each, and taking samples of the crust deposited inside the stacks. Smelter fires were extinguished on these occasions, of course, but the residual fumes were all but overpowering at close range and added to the terrors of vertigo.

James' journal entries are confined to terse notations of what was done, but his descriptions of the experiences to family and friends left no doubt that they were as terrifying as might be imagined for people who were not especially trained as steeplejacks or Alpine climbers, or born with a special "head for heights."

During the period of professional activity, James E. Talmage's family and family responsibilities continued to grow. Three more children were added to the five, four living, already born. Lucile was born on May 29, 1900. Helen May came into the world October 24, 1902, and after an interval of more than eight years John Russell arrived on February 1, 1911.

In June, 1901, the Talmages moved from the little home at 333 East Seventh South to a new and larger house at 970 First Avenue, which was purchased ready-built but previously unoccupied. At this time, the location was sufficiently far from the center of the city to provide some of the aspects of "country," or at least suburban, living. Sterling, Paul, and later Karl, raised chickens and rabbits, and for a time kept a burro, which they rode to deliver newspapers.

The new location was convenient to the new University of Utah campus on a grant of land taken from the Fort Douglas military reservation, to which the institution moved in 1900.

While the decrease in pressure which came with Dr. Talmage's resignation from the University faculty in 1907 permitted him slightly more leisure than before, including the rare privilege of spending many holidays at home, the press of professional and Church duties still occupied so much of his time that his "family life" was mostly a matter of scattered, very precious, brief occasions and a sort of direction by remote control. Most of the work and responsibility fell

The five youngest children of James E. Talmage (reading from upper left), Elsie, James Karl, Lucile, Helen May, and John Russell.

upon May, who shouldered it cheerfully although the pressure was at times severe.

One dividend of the remunerative professional work in which James engaged was the ability to let Maia and the children take summer holidays at the California beaches, where a cottage would be rented for the vacation months.

In addition to his own family responsibilities, James was called on to carry an additional load for his parents at about this time. His father's health, not robust for many years, had been steadily worsening until it became impossible for him to operate the farm, and in the summer of 1901 James purchased a home for his parents in the Provo Fourth Ward. He continued to look after their welfare through the few remaining years of their lives. Susannah Preater Talmage passed away June 3, 1906 at the age of 70, while James was en route home from an eastern trip to attend the organizational meeting of the American Museums Association. James Joyce Talmage died October 31, 1908, at the age of 66. Susa, James E.'s youngest sister who had been attending Teachers' College at Columbia University until called home at the time of her mother's passing, died April 16, 1908, so that Father Talmage's death six months later was the third to sadden the family in a little more than two years.

James accepted a number of posts of civic service in the early years of the new century. He served as president of the Utah Society for the Aid of the Sightless for many years. In 1909 he headed the Utah Historical Society, and that same year helped organize, and later served a term as president of, the Utah Health League.

James' calls to special assignments in the Church, in addition to his regular duties as a home missionary and a member of the Sunday School General Board, steadily increased during this era. His talents as a writer and public speaker were repeatedly utilized in undertakings that might stretch over weeks or months, or take him to distant places.

In February, 1900, James was appointed by the First Presidency to prepare a revised edition of the *Pearl of Great*

*Price,* one of the standard works of the Church. The revision was one of form only, to put the text into paragraphs, or verses, with references, in conformity with the other accepted scriptures. There was to be no change in wording or meaning, of course; but the restructuring of written material *without* changing its precise meaning is always a difficult and delicate task. James accepted the assignment "in a missionary spirit, without expectation of reward," but requested that a committee on revision be appointed by the First Presidency to carefully consider the work as it proceeded, step by step. A committee was appointed consisting of Elders Francis M. Lyman and Anthon Lund of the Council of the Twelve, and George Reynolds, of the First Council of Seventy.

The task was completed some two and one-half years later, and the revised Pearl of Great Price was officially accepted as a standard work of the Church by vote of the people at the final session of October General Conference in 1902.

In July, 1909, Dr. Talmage was assigned the writing of a series of lessons on the subject of the post-apostolic apostasy for use in the Mutual Improvement Associations. The undertaking developed into the writing of a small book which was published in December of the same year under the title of *The Great Apostasy.*

As was his custom when writing material to be used in Church organizations, James requested that a committee be appointed to review the work. *The Great Apostasy* text was read to a committee which included the First Presidency, Elders John Henry Smith and Orson F. Whitney of the Council of the Twelve, and Elder Joseph Fielding Smith, who would be named to the Council the following year.

In 1910, a small booklet by Dr. Talmage entitled "The Story of Mormonism" was published by the Bureau of Information on Temple Square. This was the material of the lecture James repeatedly presented to non-Mormon audiences in many places across the nation and abroad, adapted to "the ordinary style of essay." It had been published, in the original lecture form, in the *Improvement Era* and in the *Millennial Star*. Some years later James combined it with another favorite lecture subject, and as *The Story and Philosophy of Mormonism* it was published as a hardback volume.

On September 16, 1911, the anti-Mormon *Salt Lake Tribune* published "under sensational headlines" an account of the surreptitious obtaining of pictures of the interior of the Salt Lake Temple by unnamed men who were said to be in New York negotiating for their sale to chains of motion picture houses to "expose" the Temple rites. A set of pictures, technically very poor and obviously taken during the summer when the Temple was closed for the purpose of cleaning and renovation, was sent to the First Presidency by the parties who had obtained them, with a blackmailing proposal that the photographs would be returned to the Church authorities for $100,000, or shown publicly if the offer were not accepted.

The story of the blackmailing proposal, and the pictures themselves, were promptly published in the *Deseret Evening News*. Dr. Talmage wrote to the First Presidency, suggesting that a book describing the purposes of Latter-day Saint temples and the ordinances performed therein, and containing clear, high-quality photographs of both exteriors and interiors of existing temples, be published by the Church. The suggestion was approved, and Dr. Talmage was given a written commission to prepare the text of such a book. Ralph Savage, son of pioneer photographer Charles R. Savage, was appointed to take the photographs. The book was later published under the title *The House of the Lord*.

Some years earlier, in July, 1905, James had received a letter from the First Presidency requesting that he "print and publish in book form the course of lectures being delivered by you before the University Sunday School on the subject, Jesus the Christ, believing that they will prove a valuable acquisition to our Church Literature, and that the proposed work should be placed within the reach of Church members and general readers." The lecture course had been under way for more than two years at the time the letter was written and was not concluded for almost another year. It was presented before a special Sunday School class for students attending the University of Utah, held in Barratt Hall, a site facing Main Street and now covered by the great Church Office Building. The lecture series had to be interrupted periodically when Dr. Talmage was called away on special assignments, and the actual writing was further extensively postponed when James was given other specific assignments to take precedence.

One special call that came to him was to serve on the committee set up "to thoroughly examine all the evidence and references to Church doctrines and publications therein occurring, as accumulated during the Senate Committee relative to the protest against the confirmation of Senator Reed Smoot's place in the U.S. Senate." The record of the hearings in this *cause célèbre* already exceeded one thousand pages when the committee was appointed, and its members—Elder Charles W. Penrose of the Council of Twelve, Elder B. H. Roberts of the First Council of Seventy, and Dr. Talmage— faced an extensive task. James noted shortly after being named to the committee that its arduous labors, along with other responsibilities, "has reduced my sleep to about five hours a night."

Dr. Talmage was subpoenaed to appear before the U.S. Senate Committee on Privileges and Elections, sitting to consider the Smoot case, as an expert witness on Latter-day Saint doctrine.

> Among the books already introduced in evidence in the case is "The Articles of Faith" and I have had to make plain (seemingly a questionable compliment to the author that such is necessary) some of the statements there made. The imprint appearing on the title page, "Written by appointment and published by the Church" appears to give the book a place of prominence in the eyes of the committee.

Dr. Talmage was on the witness stand virtually the entire day of January 19, 1905, and was recalled for further questioning on January 24.

The Smoot hearings had developed after a group of Utah anti-Mormons had filed a petition of protest, charging that as an Apostle of The Church of Jesus Christ of Latter-day Saints, the senator-elect, Reed Smoot, would recognize the authority of the Church as superior to that of the nation, even in temporal matters. The petition also charged that the Church continued to encourage and practice polygamy in violation of its own manifesto and in defiance of the law of the land.

"Reed Smoot has been virtually lost sight of in this case; it is the Church that is assailed," James commented after appearing on the stand and hearing several days of questioning of other witnesses.

When Reed Smoot was officially confirmed as a member of the Senate in February, 1907, so long did the case drag out, Dr. Talmage joined heartily in the general rejoicing. Ironically, James' Washington testimony in the Smoot case, vigorously proclaiming the Church's official position on plural marriage, made him a target for verbal attacks and threats of physical violence from Utah apostate groups who were practicing polygamy in open defiance of the General Authorities of the Church.

In late 1911, while the book on temples was still in the course of preparation and Dr. Talmage's professional career was at its busiest, with many major cases pending, the course of his life was abruptly changed.

On December 7, 1911, James was awaiting news of an event of importance in his family life. Son Sterling, who had graduated from the University of Utah in 1909 at age 19 and later that year departed to fill a Church mission in England, had honorably completed his labors and post-mission travel on the Continent, and was scheduled to sail for home on that day. Subsequent news confirmed that he had done so, but before it reached his parents, still more important news had been received.

At 4 P.M. on the 7th, Elder Anthony W. Ivins of the Council of the Twelve called on James at his office to tell him that he had been chosen to become a member of the Council. At 11:30 A.M. on the following day, December 8, 1911, James E. Talmage was ordained an apostle at the hands of President Joseph F. Smith, with Presidents Anthon H. Lund and Charles W. Penrose, counsellors in the First Presidency, President Francis M. Lyman of the Council of the Twelve, and Elders Hyrum M. Smith, George F. Richards, and Joseph Fielding Smith of that Council assisting in the ordination.

# CHAPTER EIGHTEEN

# Early Apostolic Years— "Jesus the Christ"

From early boyhood James E. Talmage's life had been primarily Church-oriented, and he had placed his obligations as a priesthood holder above all others. His efforts and attainments in the fields of science and education had been with an eye to the building of the Church, meeting the needs of its members, and making its name known for good throughout the world. When the call came to devote full time to the duties of an apostle and to place his Church calling above all other considerations, James had no difficulty whatever in adjusting to the concept of abandoning what had been his major pursuits or to the heavy demands on time and effort; but he was almost overwhelmed by the magnitude of his responsibility in the new calling.

"Were such a position offered me, as a position in secular life might be tendered, I feel that I would shrink from the responsibility and hesitate even if I did not actually decline," he wrote on the day he first learned of the call to the apostleship, "but I hold myself ready to respond to any call made upon me by and in the priesthood."

James was chosen for the high position, fiftieth Latter-day apostle to be ordained, to fill the vacancy in the Council of the Twelve created when Charles W. Penrose was named second counsellor in the First Presidency following the death of John Henry Smith, who had held that position. President Smith died October 13, 1911, just a few days after the close of Semi-Annual Conference, and Elders Penrose and Talmage were called to their new positions within a few weeks rather than allowing the vacancy to remain unfilled until General Conference the following April.

James entered upon his new duties and responsibilities prayerfully and with humility and was deeply moved by the expressions of support he received from his many friends, from the Church membership generally, and from the press. In reviewing his feelings one week after receiving the call to the new position, he wrote:

> It is an interesting and somewhat remarkable fact that many non-members of the Church bring or send their tribute of good will. Among the early callers who came to give me assurances of good feeling and to offer congratulation, was Judge Geo. W. Bartch, formerly Chief Justice of Utah. Many attorneys with whom I have been associated in a professional capacity, and others with whom I have had friendly though non-official relationships—not members of our Church—have called or telephoned or written, and all evince the most sincere interest. Our own people have overwhelmed me with their expressions of good will. Telegrams have come from two absent members of the Council of the Twelve, Elders Heber J. Grant and Reed Smoot. Without the support of my brethren and sisters I would tremble indeed in entering upon the duties to which I have been called; but with such help, and with the assistance which the Lord alone can give, I feel both hope and encouragement.

James' time was as completely filled with his new duties as it had ever been at any epoch in his busy life. Many of the duties were in the nature of committee work, interviews with stake and ward officials, attendance at stake conferences, setting apart of missionaries to go into the field, and other similar things which are routine activities for a member of the Council of the Twelve. Each duty had its own particular significance, but most fit into a general pattern of regular duties.

There were, however, a number of special assignments given Elder Talmage outside of the routine.

He was retained in the position of director of the Deseret Museum, which he had helped guide to international recog-

James E. Talmage as he appeared about the time he was called into the Council of the Twelve. This picture of Dr. Talmage was used in connection with the presentation of the first edition of the book *Jesus the Christ*.

May Booth Talmage as she appeared at about the time
her husband was made an apostle.

nition. He was, however, relieved of the active duties of curator of the museum, and James was deeply gratified that the governing board appointed his son Sterling, who had long assisted his father in the museum operation prior to going into the mission field, to the position of curator.

James was given special appointments to represent the Church in speaking assignments in other parts of the nation, taking advantage both of his proven extraordinary talents as a public speaker and lecturer and also of his reputation in the world of science and education.

On one trip East to attend meetings of the National Association of Museums, James returned to the site of one of his eastern alma maters, Lehigh University, in Bethlehem, Pennsylvania, where an honorary doctorate of science was conferred on him. Dr. Talmage was the first graduate of the institution to have an honorary doctorate conferred upon him by the alma mater.

A memorable experience came in July, 1915, when James was appointed by the First Presidency to represent the Church at the World Congress of Religious Philosophies held in connection with the Panama-Pacific International Exposition in San Francisco.

The invitation to The Church of Jesus Christ of Latter-day Saints to provide a speaker on the program of the Congress was in itself an event of note. When similar sessions of the Congress had been held in conjunction with the Columbian Exposition in Chicago in 1893, Elder B. H. Roberts had presented himself and requested to be heard as a spokesman for The Church of Jesus Christ of Latter-day Saints and had been refused the privilege. Officials of the Congress on Religious Philosophies in 1915 privately told Dr. Talmage that they had endeavored to exclude the Latter-day Saints from that year's program also, but had been forced to the conclusion that they could not honestly do so. The basis of Mormonism was a distinct and separate religious philosophy, and not just a variation in secular detail from some other. In the end, the Congress invited presentations from the Catholics, Roman and

Orthodox; the Protestants, with a single spokesman for all Protestant sects; and the Latter-day Saints as the only representatives of Christianity. Brahmanism, Confucianism, Shintoism, Hinduism, and other distinctly different religious philosophies were also represented.

Dr. Talmage's address, entitled *The Philosophical Basis of Mormonism,* was later reprinted in full in the *Deseret News* and in the *Improvement Era.*

One of James' chief areas of activity was that of special writing assignments. The book on temples, *The House of the Lord,* was published at the end of September, 1912, and there were numerous articles for Church magazines, but Dr. Talmage's major undertaking in Church literature began in September 1914.

A decade earlier, Dr. Talmage had begun a course of lectures on the life of the Savior and the significance of His mission, delivered before a special class known as the University Sunday School. The lecture course was begun in October, 1904, was many times interrupted when Dr. Talmage was called away on various assignments, and was not concluded until the closing weeks of the academic year in 1906.

In the summer of 1905 James received a written request from the First Presidency to embody the lecture material into a book which would be published for general use in the Church. However, other specific assignments were given Dr. Talmage from time to time, postponing the carrying out of the Presidency's request concerning "Jesus the Christ," the title given to the lecture series and to the planned book.

In the late summer of 1914 James was called into consultation with the Presidency and discussion of the proposed book was renewed. On September 14, he was specifically directed to prepare the book "with as little delay as possible," and actual writing began.

In view of the interruptions to which he was subject either in his office or at home, James was provided a room in the Salt Lake Temple, where all of the writing of the book

*Jesus the Christ* was done. The manuscript was pencilled in longhand and is still in existence.

The room in the Temple where the writing was done—and it was assigned to Dr. Talmage for his writing on Church matters until the time of his death—is still frequently pointed out by Temple guides to those they are conducting through the sacred edifice, and sometimes visitors are told that the author never left the confines of the Temple during the writing of *Jesus the Christ*. This is a misstatement of fact, but an error easily understood, for the writing of the nearly-800-page book was completed in so short a time that it would appear that the author could have done nothing else except pause very briefly to eat and sleep while the work was in progress. Just seven months and five days elapsed from the time on September 14, 1914, until the concluding sentence was written on April 19, 1915.

In spite of this remarkably short time span, however, the author not only left the Temple frequently, but managed to devote many hours a day to his regular duties as a member of the Council of the Twelve. He was spared most weekend stake conference assignments, which might take several days with the travel facilities of 1914-15, but otherwise he carried his normal workload as a member of the Council. He even slept at home most nights, but his hours at home were extremely limited and his family was keenly aware of the time-pressure problem. James left very early each morning carrying a "satchel," a small black leather bag such as doctors use to carry their professional instruments, but which in Dr. Talmage's case contained several slices of homemade bread, buttered; two hard-cooked eggs; celery and fresh fruits in season; and a wedge of "sharp" cheddar cheese—his standard lunch. He returned home late, usually near midnight, for a bite of supper and a few hours sleep.

In considering the remarkably short span of time in which *Jesus the Christ* was written, it should be kept in mind that extensive research and preparatory work had been done in connection with the earlier lecture series. The basic material not only had been assembled, but also organized, the individual lectures of the earlier presentation generally corresponding to the division into chapters in book form. Furthermore, the material had been continually turned over in the author's mind during the ten-year interval, analyzed, reworked, refined, and often given additional research.

James had looked forward eagerly, almost passionately, and always prayerfully to the day when he should undertake the task of writing the book he most wanted to write. He was deeply aware of the magnitude of his task and he approached it in a spirit of reverent awe, knowing that the presentation and discussion of the life and eternal mission of the Savior of mankind was beyond any merely mortal skill and understanding, yet might be reasonably attempted with the help of the Lord. The privilege of doing the actual writing within the walls of the Temple, in the spirit of reverence and prayer which there prevailed, was appreciated with increasing fervency as the work proceeded.

As always when engaged in writing that was to be published and used by the Church, James requested and was granted the privilege of having his work reviewed by a committee. In the case of *Jesus the Christ,* the committee consisted of the full body of the General Authorities of the Church, as many of them as were able to attend sitting in on each weekly reading session. On one occasion, when President Joseph F. Smith had been in Hawaii during the discussion of an important point, it was brought back for further consideration after his return.

At the outset of the writing of *Jesus the Christ,* the First Presidency had not made a final decision on whether the book should be aimed at instructing the children of the Church, or at the mature, adult mind. On November 9, 1914, Dr. Talmage's journal entry records:

> During the afternoon attended a meeting of the First Presidency and certain invited members of the Deseret Sunday School Union Board. At this meeting, I read aloud several chapters of the book "Jesus the Christ" now in process of preparation, the purpose

being to ascertain whether the book would be properly suited to the lower or the higher grades of the theological department. As was intended the work is being prepared for our people in general, and is not adapted for use as a text book for immature students. It was decided by the First Presidency that the work be completed on the same scope and plan as heretofore followed, and that the theological department of the Deseret Sunday School Union provide their own outline for the students of the first year's work in the department.

On the same date, November 9—just five days less than two months from the start of actual writing—James recorded that since beginning work on the book "I have devoted every spare hour to that labor and have at present in written form, though not all in revised condition, twenty chapters."

References to the writing of the book are comparatively rare in the author's private journal, but whenever they appear they carry the feeling of vibrant urgency in which the task was pursued.

When free to do so, James devoted every free hour, six days a week, to the writing. On many occasions he noted that a number of Sunday hours were spent "in the Temple in Scriptural study." The wording of these journal entries is in contrast to other entries, made on legal holidays when routine activities were suspended, and notations read: "I spent the greater part of the day in the Temple, engaged in study and writing on the book. . . ." or "I devoted the day to writing on the book." The implication is clear that while Sundays might properly be devoted to study of the sacred subject of the life of the Lord, the actual work of writing was reserved to non-Sabbath hours, even under the most intensive pressure.

On April 19, 1915 was penned this significant journal entry:

> Finished the actual writing of the book "Jesus the Christ" to which I have devoted every spare hour since settling down to the work on September 14th last. Had it not been that I was privileged to do this work in the Temple, it would have been at present far from completion. I have felt the inspiration of the place and have appreciated the privacy and quietness incident thereto. I hope to proceed with the work of revision without delay.

James' sense of relief from the intense pressure under which he had been laboring was almost overwhelming, surpassed only by the feeling of joyful accomplishment and gratitude that the assignment had been carried through to conclusion without prolonged delays which might have been occasioned by illness or accident. He went to his home that evening in prayerful thankfulness, to share with his nearest and dearest the joy with which he overflowed. Maia and the children rejoiced with him, and rejoiced again for themselves in the feeling that they had regained a husband and a father they had all but "lost" during the period of intensive writing.

James' first words as he entered his home that night were to tell Maia that the basic writing was finished, and to tell also his feeling that this was the outstanding book of all he had written, or would ever write. The sacredness and majesty of the subject made it stand apart. James was awed by his own position—not in vain pride of authorship, for he had constantly sought the guiding inspiration of the Spirit of the Lord and also the counsel and criticism of all of his colleagues among the General Authorities of the Church, but in solemn, grateful recognition that he had been granted the privilege of carrying out this sacred assignment.

Maia, close to James always in spiritual understanding, sensed the breadth and depth of his joy and satisfaction and shared them with him. The two youngest children, who were also present, felt something deep and wonderful in the very air, but were incapable of appreciating its full significance. They both vividly remember some lighter and more physical incidents, such as Father's reaching into his pocket and producing handfuls of inch-long pencil stubs—he had employed a patent holder to permit him near-maximum use of each pencil—which provided fascinating playthings for months thereafter.

Much detail work still remained to be done, of course. Revisions were made, and the fully revised text was read to the First Presidency and Quorum of the Twelve, as many as were present in the city attending a series of readings beginning

April 27. When chapters were read and passed by this august committee they were given to the printer. Proofs were read and reread, by James himself along with a battery of experienced proofreaders, to eliminate typographical errors so far as they possibly could. Final proof sheets were returned to the printers on September 3, 1915, and on September 9 James recorded:

"Today I had the pleasure of presenting to the First Presidency the first three copies of the book 'Jesus the Christ' to leave the bindery."

The official announcement by the Presidency to the public said, in part:

> The book is more than a "Life of Christ" in the ordinary acceptation of that title, as it not only treats at length the narrative of our Lord's life and ministry in the flesh, together with His death, resurrection, and ascension, but deals also with His ante-mortal existence and Godship, and with His ministry in the resurrected state, both of old and in the current dispensation. The sacred subject of our Savior's life and mission is presented as it is accepted and proclaimed by the Church that bears His Holy Name.

The First Presidency's announcement also stated:

> We desire that the work "Jesus the Christ" be read and studied by the Latter-day Saints in their families, and in the organizations that are devoted wholly or in part to theological study. We commend it especially for use in our Church schools, as also for the advanced theological classes in Sunday Schools and priesthood quorums, for the instruction of our missionaries and for general reading.

The desires of President Joseph F. Smith and his counsellors, so expressed in 1915, appear abundantly to have been fulfilled. *Jesus the Christ* has been published in 38 editions in English, comprising 184,000 copies. It has been widely used in all of the areas suggested in the First Presidency's original announcement. Almost a half-century after its first publication, *Jesus the Christ* was designated as the official course of study for the priesthood quorums of the Church in 1963 and was also used as a study course by the Relief Society. Almost a decade later still, it continues to be carried by missionaries, read in Latter-day Saint homes, and used as a basis of study and reference in classes and discussion groups throughout the Church.

CHAPTER
NINETEEN

# Speaking and Writing Assignments

The dozen years following James E. Talmage's ordination as an apostle were as filled with diverse duties as any in his always-busy life. In addition to the more or less standard duties of his new calling, including assignments to attend stake conferences most weekends when he was not already travelling or engaged on some special project, James travelled throughout the United States on Church assignments that were given him because of his particular talents and experience in the fields of writing, editing, public speaking, and press relations.

In his private life, this was an epochal period of family development and James was a most concerned and devoted father. Yet during this critical period much of his parental guidance and direction had to be exercised *in absentia,* at long range, for never before—not even during the era of his near-annual trips to Europe—had he been away from home such a high proportion of the time, year in and year out.

Shortly after James was called to the Council of the Twelve, the Talmages purchased a home at 304 First Avenue, at the intersection of C Street and First Avenue, into which they moved on April 1, 1912. This was the last of their family homes, a larger house than that at 970 First Avenue to meet the requirements of the growing family; but in the pattern familiar to many people, the family "growth" soon reached a peak as children grew to maturity and moved away. Before many years, the new quarters were huge in proportion to those remaining to occupy them. In the interval, however, a great store of precious family experiences and memories was compiled.

Shortly after moving into their new home, James and May entertained the General Authorities of the Church in October, 1912, at a housewarming made forever memorable by the dedicatory prayer pronounced by President Joseph F. Smith. This made the already-precious home more impressive still, and set a solemnly joyous tone for the future years.

Of the children, Sterling was already fully mature and had recently returned from filling a mission in Britain at the time of the move into the new home, and Paul was approaching his majority, while John was still a babe in his second year. Four other children—Elsie, Lucile, Karl, and Helen—were in various stages of their school careers.

In November of 1912 the first permanent departure from the Talmage home came with Sterling's marriage to Nelle Allen and the establishment of his own home. Shortly before this event, Paul had left home on a temporary basis to take employment and, though not planned or foreseen at the time, he was never again to live at home for more than periods of relatively brief duration. Some two years after his first departure from home, Paul was called on a mission, the call coming to him through the branch of the Church at Globe, Arizona, where he was living and working at the time. He filled a mission in the Eastern States. He returned home at the end of 1916, and in June, 1917, following the United States' entry into World War I in April, Paul enlisted in the Utah National Guard. A month later, on July 18, he married Edna Marie Turner.

The four school-age children grew up together in a close family unit, with their own special pattern of living which was naturally influenced by Father's peculiar home-living pattern —his frequent prolonged absences—and temperament.

James had the full normal parental concern that the friends and companions of his children should share the same fundamental ideals and philosophy of life that he and May sought to instill in their own sons and daughters. His concern was particularly manifest in the matter of his daughters' "dates," and this led to some incidents which are amusing in retrospect but which at the time tended to put the girls in tears and make them despair of ever finding husbands.

Dr. Talmage had a warm and friendly personality when one got to know him, but there is no doubt that his outward manner may have been somewhat forbidding to a timid teen-ager, especially when the latter was being questioned about his family and background with an intensity that frequently made the panicky youngster feel that he had somehow been transported back through time and space to an ante-chamber of the Inquisition. Dr. Talmage's position as an apostle added to the fearsomeness (in the eyes of the boy being interrogated) of the situation, and even the son of a stake president, thoroughly schooled in Gospel doctrine, might be excused for stammering over questions he could have answered by rote in a Sunday School class.

The crowning blow frequently came when Dr. Talmage called on his daughter's "date" to be the voice in family prayer before the young couple set out for their evening's entertainment. This was an ordeal for even the stoutest teen-age spirit, and it is not to be wondered at that some of the boys simply collapsed and became tongue-tied under the pressure. Those who did carry through were usually so shaken that it kept them from enjoying the rest of the evening. No amount of tearful pleading by the girls, however, could ever persuade Father that he should abandon this custom, and it is understandable that the girls felt relieved that Father was so frequently away from home when their young men called.

In all fairness it should be noted that the few boys who did survive this acid test of character and courage and came back for more were made of the stuff from which heroes are fashioned, well fitted to face the problems and perils of life. All of the girls eventually found excellent husbands.

The school-age children developed a little stratagem of their own which also involved the evening family prayer circle.

Dr. Talmage was not unreasonable in his restrictions on where and with whom his children went out for evening entertainment, but he did prefer to know full details in advance.

Frequently when one or another of the children made plans at a late hour and had not had time for a discussion and the obtaining of parental approval, word would be quietly passed to the other children, and whichever one was called upon to be the voice in family prayers would insert a phrase such as:

". . . And bless Lucile who is going to the dance this evening, that she may be protected from harm and evil and return home safely. . . ."

There is no record of the success ratio in the use of this little ploy, but it was tried on many occasions, especially when Father came home unexpectedly in time for family dinner.

Dr. Talmage's frequent prolonged absences from home in connection with his Church duties had a number of side-effects on his home and family life, one of which was that he never owned an automobile. He felt that it would be unwise to have a car left in the hands of adolescents without a father's guidance, often for months at a time, and he chose to do without the convenience of a family car, even though in the early days of commercial automotive development he had numerous offers of an automobile at far below the market price, or even as an outright gift. In those days it was a common promotional practice for dealers to offer cars to men of prominence, and particularly to those with reputations in the field of science who might be presumed to understand the exciting mysteries of the internal combustion engine. The dealers, of course, counted on getting their return in advertising value. Needless to say, the Talmage children did not see eye to eye with their father on his attitude towards automobiles, but he was not to be shaken from his conviction.

While the older children could understand the reason for their father's frequent prolonged absences, the younger ones were sometimes mystified and resentful, and James notes that his four-year-old plaintively asked "why my Father can't be home like other boys' fathers are—specially at Christmas" when Dr. Talmage had to leave hurriedly for the East—his third such trip in less than three months—just a few days before Christmas in 1915.

This trip, like many others, was for the purpose of overseeing printing and publishing work for which there were then no adequate facilities in Utah. In addition to projects involving successive editions of his own writings, *Jesus the Christ* and *The Articles of Faith,* Dr. Talmage was charged with the supervision of revised-format publications of all of the scriptural standard works of the Church.

The work on revising the *Pearl of Great Price* to divide the text into paragraph form with numbered verses for convenient reference and citation, has been noted in a previous chapter.

Early in 1920, it was found that the electroplates from which the *Book of Mormon* was printed had become worn in places and that new plates should be made. It was also discovered that over the years and through the production of successive editions, some minor errors had crept in. A committee was appointed by the First Presidency to go carefully through all previous editions of the *Book of Mormon,* painstakingly comparing the several texts and eliminating all errors of printing and transcription. Dr. Talmage was a member of this committee, and was given the special assignment of checking grammar and punctuation. It was also decided to revise, expand, and unify the system of footnotes and cross-references, to precede each chapter with a brief synopsis of its contents, and to place a rule down the middle of each page, separating the text into two narrower, more easily-read columns as is done with the standard editions of the *Bible.* This also became the particular assignment of Dr. Talmage, who had the further arduous tasks of overseeing the actual production of the finished volume, making the final check of the successive proofs, passing on the quality of the paper and the binding, and attending to all the other myriad details involved in the publication of a book that is more than an ordinary volume of reading matter: a book of Holy Writ that is to carry the word of the Lord and the name of the Church to all the corners of the earth.

The new *Book of Mormon* edition was first brought out in the "missionary edition," embodying the least expensive suitable paper and binding in order to make it available at minimum cost. It was also published in a "library edition" on better quality materials for the use which the "library" name suggests, and at Dr. Talmage's suggestion a top-quality "presentation edition," in limp leather and on thin paper, was added. Dr. Talmage took great satisfaction in ordering a number of copies of this edition at his personal expense and presenting them to the First Presidency and members of the *Book of Mormon* committee with whom he had worked so long on this project.

The revised format of the *Book of Mormon* was so well received that it was decided to undertake a comparable revision of the *Doctrine and Covenants.* The old *Book of Mormon* committee was placed in charge of the project, but the committee met and decided "that instead of dividing up the work of revision as was done in the case of the *Book of Mormon,* the whole matter be left to a sub-committee of one." Dr. Talmage was that one, assigned to do the actual work, although the full committee of course retained responsibility for carefully passing on the final production.

It was also decided to publish the *Pearl of Great Price,* which had already been revised and put in numbered-verse form, in the precise style of the *Book of Mormon* and *Doctrine and Covenants,* and Dr. Talmage undertook this task concurrently with the revision of the *Doctrine and Covenants.* When the two books of scripture were published in their revised format, a new combined volume containing the *Book of Mormon, Doctrine and Covenants,* and *Pearl of Great Price* on India paper and in a single leather binding, was first produced.

Another special project relating to special Latter-day Saint use of the scriptures in which Dr. Talmage participated was the revision of a small volume known as "Ready References" to the *Bible.* The compilation of references to biblical passages relating to specific subject areas had been made by Elders George C. Lambert and Herbert L. James in 1884 and had been widely used by Latter-day Saint missionaries and students since that time. In November, 1916, Elders Joseph Fielding Smith and James E. Talmage were assigned the task of revising and expanding the little volume, which was then bound in special editions of both Oxford and Cambridge publications of the King James version of the *Bible* for use of Latter-day Saints and any others who wished to avail themselves of it. For a time after these special bindings of the *Bible* first appeared, the Oxford people abandoned the project in response to pressure from anti-Mormon groups. They later resumed production of a special edition of the *Bible* with *Ready References,* and the Cambridge people never did abandon its production in spite of pressures brought to bear on them to do so.

A writing project which had wide and lasting benefits was undertaken by Dr. Talmage about this same time and continued over a period of several years. This was a series of articles which were placed in influential newspapers in many cities across the nation, to expound the doctrines of the Church and assist the labors of the missionaries working in the areas where these newspapers circulated. After some experiments with this method during the summer of 1916, Dr. Talmage made arrangements for the publication of a regular series of articles to appear in the Sunday editions of the Boston *Post,* Philadelphia *Ledger,* Atlanta *Constitution,* and San Francisco *Chronicle,* beginning in January, 1917.

The program proved to be highly successful, although there were instances where newspaper editors succumbed to pressure from anti-Mormon groups and stopped publication, sometimes repudiating written contracts in so doing. It was found, however, that in most instances where one newspaper dropped the series, another newspaper in the same city took up the contract. At the end of the first year of publication, the articles were appearing in fourteen newspapers from coast to coast with a combined circulation of a million and a half. The newspaper articles were later compiled into a book published under the name *The Vitality of Mormonism,* which was widely used by missionaries.

Dr. Talmage made extensive speaking tours through the missions of the Church within the United States during this period, and made a point of calling on newspaper editors in principal cities, and often in smaller communities where anti-Mormon attitudes were strongly expressed. These tours were markedly successful from the points of view both of the reaction of lecture audiences and that of the press. Large live audiences were reached in cities in all parts of the nation, and most of the public addresses were extensively and fairly reported in the press, frequently in sharp contrast to previous attitudes ranging from cold disdain to outright hostility. Some newspaper editors "literally begged" to be included among those publishing the special paid series of articles, and while the profit motive is readily apparent in this attitude, it is also notable that many of these same journals had in the not-distant past adamantly refused to do anything that might in the least favor the Mormons.

During World War I, Dr. Talmage came into a special and unusual assignment that attracted national attention. An address he delivered in Ogden, defining the attitude of The Church of Jesus Christ of Latter-day Saints towards the United States' position in the world conflict, was picked up and given considerable prominence by national publications. Thereafter until the end of the war, wherever he went James was likely to be asked to speak on "Mormonism and the War," and on this topic he addressed audiences from coast to coast, some of them numbering thousands of listeners.

The progress of the great world conflict was closely followed in the Talmage home, as a matter of general patriotic interest and also for more personal reasons. Sterling was not called in the draft, being exempt as a married man, but did enter the reserves, and drilled regularly. Both Paul and Karl served in the 145th Field Artillery, the Utah National Guard unit which was commanded by Brigadier General Richard W. Young, former president of Ensign Stake, whose home was across the street from the Talmages and who was one of James and May's close personal friends. The 145th went overseas but missed going into action by less than two weeks, having received orders to go to the front within the fortnight when the armistice was signed. In addition to the two boys in the

145th, son-in-law Harold C. Brandley, who married Elsie in November, 1917, served in the Canadian Army, although he did not go overseas.

A year after the end of the War, in November, 1919, Dr. Talmage went to Pittsburgh on a special assignment that proved to be one of the most memorable of his life. For several years previously, while public and press attitudes toward the Church had been showing such marked change for the better in most parts of the nation, Pittsburgh had stood out as a hotbed of violent anti-Mormon activity. This was principally the work of a self-styled "National Reform Association" led by a Dr. Tibbetts and a Mrs. Lulu Shepard who kept a group of women's organizations in perpetual ferment and disseminated a seemingly endless stream of vicious anti-Mormon falsehoods.

The National Reform Association widely advertised a series of meetings it would sponsor in early November, 1919, under the title of the "Third World's Christian Citizenship Conference." Twenty-seven sessions were scheduled over an eight-day period, and most of the programmed discussion-subjects were in harmony with the overall conference title— e.g., "The Kingship of Christ," "The World Conscience," "The Moral Element in Public Education," "The World Commission on Social Purity," and "The World Commission on Capital and Labor." On November 12 there was scheduled a full day of discussion on "The World Commission on Mormonism."

There were numerous indications that this was not to be an objective consideration of The Church of Jesus Christ of Latter-day Saints, as might have been the case because of "Mormonism's unique philosophical basis"—as was recognized by the directors of the World Congress of Religious Philosophies in 1915—but a planned and organized attack on "Mormonism" by some of its most bigoted and violent enemies.

Dr. Talmage was appointed to represent the Church at the Pittsburgh meetings, to observe what went on, and to reply to any false charges which might be brought against the

Mormons. The entire community in Utah was concerned with this situation, and Major Wesley E. King, a distinguished non-Mormon citizen of Utah, also went to Pittsburgh to attend the conference, representing the Commercial Club (Chamber of Commerce) and Rotary Club of Salt Lake City. Major King, Dr. Talmage, and President George W. McCune of the Eastern States Mission, registered as delegates to the conference.

The early sessions of the conference were well organized and conducted, and Dr. Talmage was impressed by the "able presentation of the subjects and the liberal provision made for discussion." However, when the November 12 sessions on the "World Commission on Mormonism" opened, it was made immediately apparent that an entirely different spirit prevailed. The session chairman in his opening remarks made it plain that Mormonism was not to be examined objectively but to be broadly denounced.

A succession of trite and frequently-disproved charges against The Church of Jesus Christ of Latter-day Saints were repeated in violent terms by the early speakers, and some new charges were brought that should have collapsed from the weight of their own absurdity but which were accepted as true by a large part of the hostile audience. It was asserted that the Mormon Church had a sinister, nation-wide underground political organization that enabled it to control both houses of Congress and would permit it to decide who would be the next President of the United States; that the Mormon Church subsidized a large segment of the American press; that the existing nation-wide sugar shortage was caused by the cupidity of the Mormons, who were asserted to control both beet and cane sugar industries across the nation; that every Mormon who entered a temple of the Church was placed under oath of treasonable hostility to the government of the United States. Other comparably fantastic charges were hurled, without any pretense of offering proof, each one inciting the assembly to a higher pitch of fanatical anger.

A British female novelist who wrote under the pen name of Winifred Graham, and who specialized in lurid anti-Mormon themes, vehemently assailed the United States government and particularly the Attorney General for failing to stamp out Mormonism.

Dr. Talmage and Major King had filed written requests to be heard in accordance with published rules of the conference. In earlier meetings, similar requests from registered delegates had been courteously met, but it was again made plain that this session was being conducted in an entirely different vein and that freedom of discussion was sharply abridged.

It was announced by James S. Martin, new president of the National Reform Association, that a Mormon Apostle was in attendance and had requested to be heard, but that he had no right to be heard because the conference was a Christian gathering and—as those present were supposed to know— Mormonism was definitely un-Christian. Mr. Martin asked the gathering of 2,000 if the Mormon should be granted five minutes' time as a matter of special privilege, as he must not be allowed to speak as a matter of right.

"At this stage," Dr. Talmage noted in his report to the First Presidency, "the audience manifested infection from what one of this evening's newspapers calls 'germs of riot.'"

The "special privilege" of five minutes was granted Dr. Talmage, however, and the allotted time was used to read a letter written by Acting Governor Harden Bennion, and later fully endorsed by telegram by Simon Bamberger, Utah's first non-Mormon governor since statehood, when he returned to Salt Lake from an out-of-state trip. The letter referred to "certain press reports calculated to cast odium upon a church which comprises a majority of the citizens of Utah" and unequivocally stated that, "Having personal and official knowledge of the facts to the contrary I am issuing this general and specific denial of these unwarranted and scandalous assertions."

Dr. Talmage's reading of the letter and of Governor Bamberger's telegraphic endorsement of it was accomplished "to the accompaniment of hisses and other ridicule."

Major King, although himself a non-Mormon, was accorded no more courtesy, and his reading of a letter from the president and board of governors of the Commercial Club of Salt Lake City—many of whom were also non-Mormons—was also loudly hissed. When the Major read a letter in the same vein signed by six Salt Lake City ministers of as many Evangelical churches, there were shouts of indignation and Major King was openly accused of forging the signatures.

The mob spirit fed upon itself and increased in violence. Dr. Talmage records the proceedings and his own feelings in a journal passage which he did not incorporate in his written report to the First Presidency prepared immediately following the turbulent session, "as I prefer to inform them later, in person":

> While the turmoil and signs of threatened violence were strongest, I was impressed to the effect that the evil one had determined to arouse the mob to a murderous pitch, and specifically to bring about my death. In response to this impression, which amounted to a conviction, my soul was surcharged with the upwelling prayer-thought and intense supplication that, if a sacrifice was required or to be permitted at that time, and if I was to be the subject, it should be effected without possible excuse or extenuation based on any rash or overt act or word of mine.
>
> I was not silent, for I constantly tried to answer such of the storm of questions as I could catch; and for a time I feared that the human proneness to retaliation would assert itself and that I would display resentment and so put myself on the low plane of my assailants. I knew that the mob lacked only a leader and an excuse to fall upon me.
>
> As I prayed, there came to me a peace as well as calm. I was ready and I felt that I could give up my life without a struggle of protest. This peace abided with me.
>
> As I was hustled and jostled along the foyer toward the exit from the Mosque [the building in which the Conference on Mormonism was held was named the Syria Mosque because of its architectural form], the mob seemed to lose sight of me. For the last few yards I walked in the midst of the throng, untouched by all. I saw several people looking for me in bewilderment, and heard uttered inquiries of, "Where is he?", etc. President McCune handed me my overcoat and hat, which I leisurely donned along with muffler and gloves, and then descended the steps to the street.

Brother McCune had been near me from the time I left the auditorium. I learned from him that while I was surrounded on the stage, a crowd in the foyer was plotting to seize me as I would leave. President McCune mingled with the throng and dissuaded them in part. He had risen in the conference session and made motions and offered seconds to other motions, but was known to the assembly only as a representative from Brooklyn [and not as one of the Mormons].

I enter here my firm belief, based on impressions received during this day, that blood of the members of this Church will yet be shed through persecution at the hands of professing Christians and in further testimony of the Gospel of Jesus Christ.

James' life was again severely threatened in a different way within a few weeks of the Pittsburgh experience.

Dr. Talmage went through Arkansas and Texas with President Samuel O. Bennion of the Central States Mission. A prolonged sub-zero cold spell, combined with a severe shortage of natural gas, the standard space-heating fuel of that area, brought both men down with severe colds and sore throats. Dr. Talmage, continuing to meet a taxing schedule of speaking engagements, developed a lung congestion which turned into acute bronchial pneumonia.

He completed his speaking tour, but was in a state of near-collapse when he and President Bennion returned to mission headquarters in Independence, Missouri, on December 18. James was confined to bed for weeks and May was summoned from Salt Lake, as his life hung in the balance. It was late January before he was sufficiently recovered to return home and many more months before he could perform the slightest exertion without strain, but eventually his recovery was complete.

The years of the early 1920's continued to be filled with a variety of official duties and events of personal interest for James E. Talmage. Grandchildren brought a fresh thrill into the lives of their grandparents, as is always the case. James and May first became grandparents on September 22, 1918, when Elsie (Mrs. Harold C. Brandley) became the proud and happy mother of twin girls. Paul's wife Edna had a child,

In June, 1922, James E. Talmage received an honorary Doctorate of Laws from Brigham Young University. Awaiting the forming of the official procession are, left to right, Dr. John A. Widtsoe, Dr. Talmage, Joseph Fielding Smith, Charles W. Penrose, President Heber J. Grant, David O. McKay (who received an honorary Master of Arts degree that same day), Stephen L Richards, and Richard R. Lyman.

also a girl, on March 2, 1919, and Elsie added to the number of granddaughters from time to time—she and Harold eventually had a family of seven children, all girls. The first grandson was brought into the family on February 7, 1921, by Lucile, who had married Wilford C. Carlisle of Logan and moved to Berkeley, California.

The severe economic recession which followed the World War I "boom" was keenly felt but successfully weathered in the Talmage family. Helen continued her college career, and Sterling fulfilled a long-cherished ambition of himself and of his father when he went to Lehigh University, James' alma mater, to obtain a master's degree in mining engineering in 1923. Sterling went on to Harvard University the following autumn, obtaining his doctorate in the field of geology in 1925. Sterling spent his final year at Harvard as recipient of the Emmons Memorial Fellowship in economic geology, an honor which brought as much happy pride to his father as to himself.

James himself received additional academic recognition in the early 1920's. Honorary degrees of Doctor of Laws were conferred on him by Brigham Young University and the University of Utah, two institutions where so much of his own career in education had been spent, within the same week, in June, 1922.

In August, 1924 a major change in assignment came when James E. Talmage was called to preside over the British and European Missions of the Church. The assignment came somewhat as a surprise, as President David O. McKay had been presiding over these missions for a little less than two years (President McKay had developed some health problems which made it advisable for him to return home), and Dr. Talmage was called to the post slightly out of the order of seniority which had generally been followed.

# The European Mission

On October 15, 1924, James E. Talmage boarded the so-familiar train eastbound from Salt Lake City, beginning a journey that was in many respects unique even though a retracing of an oft-travelled route. He was accompanied by Maia and by his two youngest children, Helen and John, and it was a source of keen delight to have them share the travel experiences and visit places of interest which James had many times described to them. It was a curious fact, too, that in a lifetime so largely devoted to Church work, including so many special assignments which he was instructed to regard as "mission" calls, James had never before gone out from Zion to "fill a mission" in the narrower and more commonly accepted meaning of that phrase among Latter-day Saints: the devoting of full time to proselyting and related Church activities for a two- or three-year period in a designated geographical area.

The Talmage family arrived at Liverpool aboard the Canadian Pacific liner *Montcalm* on the evening of October 31, and President David O. McKay was at the quay to greet the travellers and transport them through the rainy, misty English darkness in a Model "T" Ford to what was to be their home for the next three years: Durham House, 295 Edge Lane, Liverpool, headquarters of the British and European Missions of the Church.

Discussions with President McKay, who stayed for six weeks after the Talmages' arrival to discuss mission affairs, quickly made the new mission president acquainted with many of the principal problems he would be facing. Some of them did not need to be explained. Indeed, they were literally shouted, if not from the housetops, at least in the principal streets, and blazoned in letters two inches high on the placards commonly used to promote the sale of British newspapers.

The press throughout Britain was engaged, and had been for a long time, in a campaign of vilification against the Mormons that was shocking in an age of enlightenment and free transmission of news around the globe. Leading daily and weekly newspapers—with some exceptions which disdained to descend to such depths of yellow journalism but which ignored the Mormons completely and did nothing to correct the false impression created by their confreres—carried lurid tales about the Mormons and their alleged debaucheries with polygamous wives and numerous concubines. The Latter-day Saint missionary system was pictured to readers of these sensational stories as an intricately organized white-slave operation which was taking innocent British girls away to far-off Utah, depicted as the Sodom and Gomorrah of modern days, to be forever condemned to lives of horror and misery.

"My Mormon Marriage"—a completely fictional piece of sensational filth but purporting to be a first-person, factual account of the awful experiences of a British girl who had been lured to Utah and later managed to escape—was a typical example of what was being carried in the irresponsible sector of the British press.

"Mormon Mysteries Unveiled—A Girl's Awful Revelations—see tonight's *Argus*," screamed the advertising placards for the Bradford (Yorkshire) *Argus*, a particularly painful thorn in the side of Latter-day Saint missionaries in that area.

In cosmopolitan and sophisticated London, a play called "Eve and the Elders," a dramatization of a novel by the same Winifred Graham who had played such a prominent role in the Pittsburgh "World Conference on Mormonism" in 1919, was in the midst of a long run on the stage.

Curiously enough, a large part of this widespread attack on the Mormons did not appear to be an organized effort on the part of the enemies of The Church of Jesus Christ of

One of the first missionary conferences conducted after James E. Talmage arrived in England to preside over the British and European Missions in 1924. President David O. McKay had not yet left the mission field to return home, and he and Mrs. McKay are included in the picture.

Latter-day Saints—although the dedicated anti-Mormons were taking every advantage of it, of course—but rather a device to promote the sale of newspapers. A certain class of reader avidly devoured this type of sensationalism. Editors published it to boost circulation, sometimes without thought or concern as to its truth or falsity or the effect of their action on an innocent people. Indeed, Mission authorities had encountered at least one sub-editor who freely admitted that his own daughter had travelled in the United States, visited Utah and seen the Latter-day Saints in their home environment, and knew how completely false were the fabricated tales being published in Britain.

"But they aid us in selling an enormous number of newspapers," the sub-editor said candidly.

The big difficulty in trying to combat this problem of the press, President McKay explained to his successor, was that Mission authorities had been unable to reach the men at the decision-making level of the offending journals. When Latter-day Saints called at the various newspapers to protest, they were invariably received by sub-editors or staff reporters who listened in cold politeness, promised to "see if something could be done," but pointedly emphasized that they themselves had no authority to order a change and would have "to take the matter up" with someone higher in the chain of command. Always the man at the top, the man who made policy, was unavailable—for a variety of reasons or, rather, of conventional fictions.

One of the reasons for Dr. Talmage's call to preside over the European Missions at this particular time was the wide experience he had acquired, and the impressive record of success he had compiled, in dealing with anti-Mormon attacks in the American press. It was hoped that he could be correspondingly successful in Britain. Another factor which was undoubtedly weighed in making the selection of a successor to President McKay as mission president, was the prestige which Dr. Talmage carried in Britain as a member of distinguished British scientific societies. President McKay had vivid recollections of the famous lecture tour of 1898 when as a young missionary he had staged Dr. Talmage's remarkably successful Glasgow appearance, and he knew the special weight which Dr. Talmage's British honors carried in their homeland. Events proved that both of these factors—experience in dealing with the press and the special prestige of membership in distinguished British institutions—were to play important roles in bringing about a spectacular change in the attitude of the British press towards the Mormons, with great benefit to the missionary effort.

James' first direct encounter with the hostile press confirmed in every detail what he had been told. The *Argus,* a daily newspaper in the city of Bradford, Yorkshire, was engaged in an all-out campaign against the Mormons. This was not merely the publication of sensational anti-Mormon fiction as a circulation-booster, but also a continuing editorial attack on The Church of Jesus Christ of Latter-day Saints as an institution and particularly on the Church's missionary labors in Bradford and vicinity.

In November, 1924, the situation in Bradford was approaching a climax, centered on the issue of the Mormon missionaries' use of the public baths of the city, on a rental basis, for performing baptisms. The *Argus* had taken the lead in a campaign to deny the Mormons use of the municipal baths, and other newspapers including the *Yorkshire Observer, Bradford Daily Telegraph,* and *Leeds Mercury* participated in the anti-Mormon campaign.

City officials, however, had taken the stand that the Latter-day Saints were breaking no laws, were abiding by the rules, were paying the standard rental fee, and were entitled to use the public facilities. Because of the newspaper agitation, the question was brought up for reconsideration, and a public hearing scheduled for November 24.

The *Argus,* seething with anger, published a scathing editorial on November 18. In it Mormonism was labelled "an abominable thing . . . an insidious attempt to sow the seeds of license in the minds of immaturity . . ." that "should be stamped out ruthlessly."

The editorial criticized city officials for not being present or represented at Mormon baptismal services for which they rented the public baths, noting that the city was always officially represented at sanctioned boxing matches. The diatribe concluded with the contrived suggestion that the exercise of boxing "would come into effect with peculiar value when the Mormon missionary is around."

The regular Latter-day Saint conference in this area of the British Mission was scheduled for the weekend prior to the municipal baths hearing, and Dr. Talmage went to Yorkshire a few days early in an effort to talk to the editors of the hostile newspapers.

Accompanied by President John E. Wahlquist of the Leeds Conference [District] and other missionaries laboring in the area, James presented himself at the offices of the several newspapers and met precisely the reception he had been warned to expect. When he offered his calling card, it was taken to the editor (or a pretense was made of doing so) only to be brought back with the professedly regretful announcement that the editor's schedule was so filled that he could not possibly find time for an interview with the visitor.

Dr. Talmage then resorted to a little stratagem which he had been mulling over in his mind and which only he among the authorities of The Church of Jesus Christ of Latter-day Saints could have adopted.

James would ask the newspaper staffman if he might have his calling card back for a moment to add a note which he had earlier "forgotten" to append. Taking his pen he wrote after his name: F.R.S.E., F.R.M.S., F.R.G.S.—signifying "Fellow of the Royal Society of Edinburgh," "Fellow of the Royal Microscopical Society," "Fellow of the Royal Geological Society."

The effect on the several British newspapermen was electric. These were designations with which they were familiar and of which the significance did not have to be explained. The cryptic notations carried a potent message: the owner of these titles was no ordinary American, but a man recognized and honored by prestigious *British* institutions. Fellowship in the Royal Society of Edinburgh was especially impressive at this particular time, for the Prince of Wales—an untarnished national idol in 1924—was to be given honorary R.S.E. fellowship within a few weeks, and the institution was very much in the news.

The newspapermen to whom the altered calling cards were returned gave a startled glance at the inked initialings and hastily excused themselves to return for a further discussion with their editors. Almost always they returned with word that the editor had, after all, managed to squeeze a few minutes from his crowded schedule, either immediately or at some specified time in the near future.

Once through the previously impregnable door to the editor's *sanctum sanctorum,* James had most of his battle won. Face to face with an educated and generally reasonable man who had authority to act, it was a relatively simple task to convince him of the unfairness and lack of journalistic integrity in the unwarranted attacks on the Mormons—particularly when the speaker possessed such impressive credentials in the way of British scientific honors. Dr. Talmage's long experience in dealing with newspaper editors on the other side of the Atlantic was also extremely helpful.

The immediate effect of the visits to editorial offices in the Bradford-Leeds area was the appearance of generally fair and objective reports of the LDS conference sessions in most of the area dailies, and the promise of a complete reconsideration of policy toward the Mormons in the future. Dr. Talmage was unable to see the editor of the *Argus* at this time, as he was genuinely ill, but James wrote a substantial article replying to that newspaper's charges, and extending an invitation to Bradford municipal authorities and others, including the *Argus'* own representatives, to witness the Mormon baptismal ceremonies. This he delivered to the second-in-command, and in the issue of November 24 the communication appeared in full, some 24 column-inches of type under a two-column headline reading, "Letter from Mormon Apostle—Categorical Denials of Leader of European Missions—Bradford Baptisms—Witnesses Invited to Baths Ceremonies."

The conference meetings were unusually well attended, the audience at the evening session being counted at 472. Dr. Talmage noted that "but for the newspaper agitation we would have had no such numbers."

On the day following the conference meetings, the public hearing on the Mormons' use of the municipal baths was held. City authorities treated Dr. Talmage and the other Latter-day Saint missionaries courteously and gave them full opportunity to state their case. When the vote was taken, it was nine to two in favor of allowing the Latter-day Saints to continue using the municipal baths. The following morning's *Yorkshire Observer* carried a headline proclaiming "Victory for the Mormons."

Similar headlines appeared in other newspapers, including the London dailies, for the Bradford Baths issue had become something of a *cause célèbre* throughout the nation. Some of the press accounts carried the implication that the "Mormon victory" was a defeat for British morality, but a first crack had been made in the solid wall of newspaper hostility toward the Latter-day Saints.

Over the next few months, Dr. Talmage made calls on other newspaper editors across Britain, giving first priority to those which had exhibited the strongest anti-Mormon bias, but making a point of calling on the press wherever he went on Mission business.

The campaign was astonishingly successful. Within a few months, anti-Mormon attacks in the British press—a real problem for Latter-day Saint missionaries laboring in Britain for many years—had become the exception rather than the rule. By 1926, they were a genuine rarity, and when they did occur it was almost always possible to obtain a prompt retraction and apology. In June, 1927, an anti-Mormon article appeared in the *World Pictorial News* published in Manchester. The article was based on the statements of a man named William Ernest Bowns, who represented himself as a former "Mormon Elder" and had even gone to the trouble of forging certificates of Church membership and ordination which he used to convince the *Pictorial News* editors of his *bona fides.*

When the deception was exposed, the syndicate controlling the *World Pictorial News* took prompt action to rectify the mistake and specifically requested that Dr. Talmage write an article refuting Bowns' sensational charges. This article was duly published and given equal prominence with that which had been accorded Bowns' story.

James wrote:

> Perhaps this is the first time in the history of the British Mission that the chief official of a great newspaper syndicate has sent a representative to the Mission president really asking for conciliation and expressing deep regret for what has been said against us in their newspapers. I can well understand that the newspapers took up Bowns' story because he was speaking in the first person, and professing to give a first-hand account of what he had experienced.

The change in the attitude of the press was not reflected only in the disappearance of scurrilous anti-Mormon attacks but also in positive ways, including objective reporting of Latter-day Saint activities and even occasional articles directly praising the Mormons and their work.

A high point in the press relations campaign came early in 1926, when through the good offices of Ralph J. Pugh, a prominent London businessman and active Latter-day Saint, Dr. Talmage met with Lord Beaverbrook and Viscount Castlerosse. Lord Beaverbrook was one of the giants of the British press, owner of the London *Daily Express* and *Sunday Express* and many other newspaper enterprises. Viscount Castlerosse was a leading Roman Catholic, a prominent member of the House of Lords, and well known public figure throughout Britain.

As a result of the meeting, a two-hour discussion during which the British peers asked and had answered scores of penetrating questions about The Church of Jesus Christ of Latter-day Saints and its missionary system, there appeared in the *Sunday Express* of February 14, 1926, an article under the by-line of Viscount Castlerosse with the heading "Fair Play for the Mormons." It refuted many of the popular calumnies against the Mormons, praised the sincerity, industry, and integrity of the Latter-day Saints, and had great effect in countering the few remaining voices raised in violent opposition to the Mormons and their missionary efforts in Britain.

Over the years since Dr. Talmage's term as European Missions president, relations between the Church and the press in Britain and other European countries have continued to improve. Many people have contributed to the improvement, but the changes brought about in 1924-1927 under James E. Talmage's direction remain a landmark in this area of endeavor. There have since been, and perhaps always will be, periodic isolated anti-Mormon outbursts, but in nearly half a century there has been nothing even approaching the vitriolic attacks that characterized the nineteen-teens and early 1920's.

As president of British and European Missions, Dr. Talmage of course had a multitude of important duties in addition to his efforts to eradicate anti-Mormon prejudice from the British press. He travelled the length and breadth of the British Isles to attend the district conferences and to lend support and counsel to the missionaries in the field. He made periodic visits to the missions in continental Europe, and was sometimes absent from Liverpool headquarters for months at a time.

A substantial effort went into a campaign to upgrade the quality of the meeting places of Latter-day Saints in the missions. In only a few places did the saints own their own chapels or improvised meeting halls, and most of these were lamentably run down and poorly situated. Many changes for the better were effected and the missionary effort benefitted.

In the summer of 1925, Dr. Talmage presided over the

In the summer of 1925 James E. Talmage visited the home of his great friend and teacher, Karl G. Maeser, in Meissen, Germany, and arranged to have a commemorative plaque placed on the building.

first major change in mission boundaries in many years. The Swiss-German Mission, comprising all of the German-speaking territories of Europe, was divided into two missions. One was thereafter known as the Swiss-German Mission with headquarters in Basel, Switzerland, and the other designated as the German-Austrian Mission with headquarters in Dresden, German. These territorial boundaries have since been subdivided.

During the course of travels through Germany, James had the deep pleasure and satisfaction of visiting the birthplace of his one-time teacher and great friend Karl G. Maeser, in Meissen, a suburb of Dresden. Arrangements were made for the placing of a permanent commemorative plaque on the house where Dr. Maeser was born, and James presided at its installation during a subsequent visit to the German missions in 1926.

One of James' real delights was to have Maia accompany him to places which he had many times described to her over the years. As presiding officer over Relief Societies in the missions, May had her own official duties to perform.

In 1926, on an extended trip which took them to the Scandinavian countries, James and May made what may have been the first use of commercial aviation for mission travel. They took a scheduled flight from Amsterdam to Copenhagen, and found it an exciting and exhilarating experience, despite bouts of air sickness and some nose-bleeding occasioned by rapid changes in altitude. They were impressed that the Ford tri-motor plane made the 400-mile trip in just a little over four hours actual flying time, not counting one 40-minute stopover in Hamburg. James noted that "all eight seats in the plane were occupied." The size of the payload tells its own story concerning the difficulties of conducting pioneer commercial air operations.

In spite of the very extensive travel required in the conduct of mission affairs, James found opportunities for "home life" at mission headquarters that he had not known since the early days of his marriage. When he was in Liverpool he had his office in the same building as his living quarters, and this meant that he appeared at table for three meals a day, conducted the pre-breakfast scripture-study classes, and took time for after-dinner talks with the "mission family"—comprising, as well as members of his own family, the splendid young men called from the field to fill the staff positions of associate editor of the *Millennial Star* and mission secretary and treasurer. Sometimes Dr. Talmage could be prevailed upon to read to the group after dinner, frequently from the book of verse *Pearls of the Faith,* translated from the Persian. To his children, it was a continuing source of marvel and delight, "every day a holiday," for at home in Utah it had been only a scattering of special holidays when Father had been able to take time for such simple domestic pleasures. It is probable that James' youngest son had more actual contact with his father during the years in Liverpool than in all the rest of his life.

While Dr. Talmage found joy and satisfaction in his mission labors and there were brief periods of relaxation, the heavy pressures and demands imposed by his many duties and extensive travels took their toll and he became increasingly worn, physically, as time went by. In the late winter of 1926 James had a recurrence of the bronchial pneumonia which had so nearly taken his life in Independence, Missouri, in 1919-20. For four weeks he lay in bed, hovering between a vague semi-consciousness and outright delirium, but at no time did he have any feeling that his life might be taken at this time, a feeling that had been strong on a number of previous occasions of serious illness. He was sufficiently recovered by the end of March to return to his duties.

In the winter of 1927 James slipped on an icy patch of pavement in Glasgow, falling heavily and injuring his left knee. The injury was aggravated a short time later by another fall, this time on a loosened carpet on the stairs at mission headquarters, and from that time forward James was in constant pain which became increasingly severe with the passage of time. He refused to take time from his mission labors to go into a hospital, believing that this could be postponed until

he returned to Utah. Stoically, he said little about his affliction, and forced himself to take regular long walks to exercise the injured member, although these were excruciatingly
painful.

Late in the summer of 1927, James left on his final mission
tour, which would take him through Central Europe to Syria,
where Elder Joseph Wilford Booth and his wife Rebecca were
conducting Church affairs among a group of Armenian refu-
gees whose circumstances were truly pitiful. Elder Booth was
May's brother, and was filling his fourth mission to this part
of the world. James had long planned and looked forward
to this visit, but when the time came to embark on it his joy
was tempered by worry over his physical condition and his
ability to withstand the rigors of prolonged travel, especially
in the somewhat primitive conditions prevailing through the
Middle East.

James arrived in Aleppo, Syria, on October 10 after two
months of steady travel, which saw him visit the French, Swiss,
and German Missions along the way and then pass through
Budapest, Belgrade, Sofia, and Istanbul. He had a joyous
reunion with his brother- and sister-in-law and spent the following week among the Armenian Latter-day Saints observing
the conditions in which they lived, studying their problems,
and preparing recommendations to be sent to the First Presidency. The recommendations were concerned both with the
best ways of assisting these destitute people to provide for
themselves and the conduct of future missionary labors in this
part of the world.

While in Aleppo, James received a cablegram from Liverpool headquarters, relaying the word received there that Dr.
John A. Widtsoe had been named to succeed him in the European Mission presidency at an early date. The depth of James'
physical weariness and pain is clearly seen in the brief comment recorded in his journal:

"And so, the release or transfer of wife and myself to the
home field is within sight. I am grateful."

After completing his official mission tasks, and before
starting the return journey, James fulfilled a long-cherished

dream by visiting Jerusalem and the biblical lands around it. This is one of life's memorable experiences to every devout Christian or Jew fortunate enough to experience it, but for James it had a special dimension and depth of meaning beyond the norm. His years of study and research and his reverent and prayerful writing of the earthly ministry of the Son of God had made this part of the world almost a part of his life, although he had never actually seen it. Countless times he had closed his eyes and called on inspired imagination to depict the scenes where the mighty drama of the Meridian of Time had unfolded, and now to stand in the sacred and historic places, to see the landscapes that had been familiar to the mortal Jesus, and to Abraham and all the line of Old Testament prophets, filled him with joyous wonderment and prayerful thankfulness for the experience beyond the capacity of words to express.

Accompanied by President Booth, James entered Palestine on October 11 and went to Nazareth, boyhood home of the Savior and site of the beginning of His ministry. From there they went to the Sea of Galilee, on which they took a short excursion in a boat that probably differed little from those used by Peter and John, the fishers who left them to become fishers of men. They stood on the shores of the Dead Sea and tasted its extremely bitter brine, and they followed the course of the River Jordan.

In Bethlehem they saw the grotto, or stable, which is purportedly the actual site of Jesus' birth—now "embellished, laden with gold, and hung with votive lamps." In Jerusalem they found many similarly elaborate shrines at places claimed to be precisely those where occurred the historic events in the life of the Christ and of His terrible death by crucifixion. James' brief journal entries carefully note that many such places are "claimed" or "purported" to be the precise spots where various events occurred and that they had been converted into elaborate tourist shrines. He was not concerned with questions of exact location or of man-made changes. He stood in the places where the Savior had passed in His mortal life, saw the horizons which had marked His familiar world, and was forever grateful.

When Dr. Talmage turned his face westward to return to mission headquarters he went by way of Egypt, pausing to visit the great pyramids of Gizeh and the museums of Cairo. He was fascinated with their monuments and mementos of a great ancient civilization, but his increasing infirmity was further impressed upon him when he visited the pyramids and "regretted all day my old-time ability to climb and clamber." At the end of five days in Egypt, James took passage by ship for Marseilles, from where he proceeded to Liverpool by the most direct route.

The few remaining weeks in the mission field passed rapidly in discharging official duties that had piled up during his absence, attending to current responsibilities, and making a few farewell visits, including a final trip to Hungerford and Ramsbury on which Maia accompanied him, to see the place of his birth and scenes of his childhood—she for the first time and he for the last.

Dr. Widtsoe arrived in Liverpool on Christmas Eve, and the holiday week was largely spent in acquainting him with the detail of mission operations and current problems. The mission presidency was officially passed to Dr. Widtsoe on January 1, 1928.

On January 3, James and May—there were only the two of them for the return journey, for Helen had returned home in 1925 to marry Roland Parry, and John had left a few months before his parents in order to begin the 1927-28 school year in Utah—left Liverpool for the last time. They proceeded to London and embarked on the SS *President Roosevelt* of the United States Lines on January 5.

With only brief pauses in New York, which May had never before seen, in Washington where Helen was now living with her husband and baby daughter Gloria, and in Chicago to see Sterling who was on the faculty of Northwestern University at nearby Evanston, they travelled directly to Utah, arriving in Salt Lake City on February 1, 1928.

# The Wonders of Radio

First days and weeks following the return from the European Missions were for James E. Talmage a peculiar blend of many feelings that at times created a personal world of almost unreality.

There was the joy of homecoming, the welcoming of family, friends, and associates that was "literally overwhelming," James noted, in its warmth and intensity and succession of special receptions and parties. Yet at the same time, the joy of homecoming was tempered by the changes that had occurred to make "home" something subtly different from what he and May had known and remembered. The family residence at 304 First Avenue was shockingly different, having been converted into five small apartments which were being managed by daughter Elsie and her husband. James and May had known and approved of the alteration, but seeing and experiencing the change was something else. It was no longer "home," but a house filled with strangers.

Shortly after their return, James and May, along with John, now the only one of the children living "at home," moved into the Hotel Utah for the remainder of the off-season for tourist travel, no one of the converted apartments in the family dwelling proving really suited to their needs. There was also the factor of convenient proximity to the Church Office Building, a matter of real and increasing importance, considering James' painful knee problem.

People as well as places had changed during the years of absence. Visits to friends and relatives showed the passage of time in the faces of loved ones, and there were gaps in the ranks. Most sorrowful of these was that caused by the absence of George Talmage, James' youngest brother, who had passed away in November, 1926, from a heart ailment from which he had long suffered.

The deep, numbing tiredness that had been steadily increasing since the debilitating falls in Glasgow and Liverpool was intensified by the crowded schedule of official, family, and social activities immediately following homecoming; and as soon as the most pressing obligations had been taken care of, James entered the LDS Hospital for a complete medical examination and extended rest.

Word from the doctors was not reassuring, although at this time strong hope of full eventual recovery was held out. The injury which James had suffered was such that the exercise he had persisted in taking in the belief that it would help preserve muscle tone until such time as proper medical treatment could be administered, had actually had an opposite effect and done severe damage. The muscles of his left thigh had been largely worn away and gave him very little support. A course of combined electrotherapy and massage was prescribed and begun, with the aim of stimulating circulation and restoring the wasted muscle tissue.

At first, James carried on with a more or less normal schedule of duties, travelling to stake conferences in the familiar pattern and filling other routine duties. A number of severe falls, all acutely embarrassing and some of them highly dangerous, brought a gradual reduction and eventual complete discontinuation of James' travel assignments. He keenly missed participating in these long-familiar activities and sometimes felt that he was not fulfilling his obligations in the office to which he had been called, but he accepted his affliction with patience and concentrated on the duties which he could perform.

A new and interesting assignment, one which was to be a major item in his work through most of the remaining years of his life, was given to Dr. Talmage in the late summer of 1928. In keeping with the Church policy of taking advantage of every development that could be adapted to the spreading of the Gospel message, the relatively new technique of radio broadcasting was adopted as a means of reaching a larger and more widespread audience than had previously been available to one speaker at one time. General Conference services were broadcast from the Tabernacle starting in the early 1920's and later a "Mormon Hour" program was inaugurated as a regular Sunday evening feature over Station KSL. Dr. Talmage first heard the radio program on August 26, 1928, when Elder John M. Knight delivered the address. Shortly afterward it was decided to present organized series of talks, developing specific themes. James E. Talmage was assigned to write and deliver the first such series, on the life and mission of Christ, and he began this pleasant task in September. This initial series of radio addresses continued through the remaining weeks of 1928 and proved so successful that Dr. Talmage was appointed to deliver a second series, through the first quarter of 1929.

When this series of talks was completed, Elder B. H. Roberts of the First Council of Seventy took over on the scheduled Sunday evening hour over Station KSL, and Dr. Talmage went to Los Angeles for a time, where he presented his earlier radio series over Radio Station KEJK in that city.

He returned to Salt Lake City in late September, 1929, and early in 1930 began another radio series over KSL. This series, by decision of the Church Radio Committee, was published weekly in small pamphlet form and sent to missionaries in all of the LDS missions around the world. It continued through the full calendar year 1930, the year after the Centennial Observance of the organization of the Church on April 6, 1830.

At the beginning of 1931, the Sunday night speaking appearance was taken over by Elder Bryant S. Hinckley, then president of Liberty Stake, who later was called to the Council of the Twelve. Dr. Talmage was given a prolonged respite from the KSL assignment following the year-long series in 1930, but was to present one more series of radio addresses in 1933. The several series of radio talks were bound into hard-back volumes under the title *Sunday Night Talks* and widely used in the missionary service.

James and May were deeply saddened during the post-mission period by deaths in the immediate families. President J. Wilford Booth of the Armenian Mission, whom James had visited in Syria and Palestine in late 1927 and who was scheduled to return to Utah after a total of 18 years' missionary labor in the Middle East, died very suddenly in December, 1928, in Aleppo, Syria. And in January of 1931, Wilford C. Carlisle, husband of daughter Lucile, died while undergoing an operation for the removal of a stomach ulcer, in Berkeley, California. Lucile and her two children returned to Utah for a time, but later went back to California.

About this time, in early 1931, radio began to play a new role in the life of James E. Talmage. While up to this time his principal contact with radio had been as a means of projecting his voice to a vast audience spread over hundreds of thousands of square miles, now it took on a new importance in his life as a means of bringing to him events beyond the range of his limited mobility.

In February, 1931, James followed the Sunday Tabernacle services by radio instead of attending in person. He did so with reluctance, but in accordance with advice from both doctors and his brethren in the councils of the Church, and with his own best judgment. The strain of climbing steps was severe, and the steps in the Tabernacle were particularly hazardous, being very steep and without handrails or any other support. Shortly prior to reaching the decision to remain at home and listen to the broadcast of the services, James had suffered a severe fall while descending the Tabernacle steps, although he had been supported by someone on each side of him. This fall, in front of an audience of thousands, had been deeply humiliating and had inflicted physical damage that he felt for many weeks. A critical and alarming aspect of such accidents was their suddenness and complete unpredictability. *Both* of James' legs were now afflicted and subject to giving way without the slightest warning.

From this time on, it became James' custom to follow the Sunday Tabernacle services by radio rather than in person. He did make public appearances on occasion, at General Conferences and to meet special speaking engagements—as, for example, the exercises incident to the closing of LDS College in late May, 1931—but he was forced to avoid such things as much as possible.

As the physical affliction became progressively worse, James took to spending two or three days at a time in his office, sleeping on a couch and having the little food of which he partook brought in to him in the worn and familiar black satchel which he had carried during the crowded days of writing *Jesus the Christ*. To keep in touch with the outside world, especially during such major events as the turbulent political campaign of 1932, James rented a small, table-top model radio for his office. He found it so useful that the family made him a present of a similar instrument.

The practice of spending extended periods in the office became more and more a way of life as the year 1932 went by and 1933 came into being. Through some oversight, the magnificent Church Administration Building at 47 East South Temple has no ground-level entrance, and to go in or out of the structure it is necessary to pass by either the broad, open front steps or the steep but narrow and handrail-guarded stairs to the back entrance. Once inside, there is elevator service to all floors, of course. But to get in or out of the building entails a passage of stairs which is a genuine hazard to one in the situation of Dr. Talmage in 1932-33 and he avoided it when he could.

Although James' physical world tended to shrink progressively as his mobility became more and more restricted, until it largely seemed to be packed into the suite of offices in the northeast corner of the second floor of the Church Administration Building, in another way it expanded to encompass the four corners of the earth. Through the wonders of radio, James could turn a knob, adjust a dial, and then with closed eyes but fully open mind and imagination, be in the midst of the events that were shaping the history of the world.

Into the room came the voice of the new President of the United States, Franklin D. Roosevelt, which was becoming so familiar to Americans everywhere and would forever stand as a sort of hallmark of the days of the Great Depression. From far-off Germany came another new and strangely frightening voice, the rage-packed scream of Adolf Hitler that was the harbinger of the holocaust that would engulf the world in the coming decade of the 1940's. The day-to-day events, sometimes tragic, sometimes comic, sometimes dramatic, and sometimes banal, brought the taste and feel of the changing world into the room. The man who had travelled so much could no longer go to far places, but he could reach out and bring the world to him.

Dr. Talmage's assigned duties could, of course, mostly be performed within the building. When it was necessary to go out, as to the weekly meetings of the Councils in the Temple, he proceeded with slow caution and the help of his brethren.

In June of 1933 Dr. Talmage began another series of Sunday night radio addresses, a treatment of the subject of Priesthood, which was to be the capstone to the monument of written and spoken words which had been built by him over the years.

# James E. Talmage—The Man

In the late 1960's, a young supermarket employee who noted the name "Talmage" on a check presented to be cashed, inquired whether the bearer were descended from "the man who wrote the Church books." The young man was dumbfounded to learn that the writer of the check was not just a "descendant" but a son of James E. Talmage.

"Why, I thought Apostle Talmage lived back in Brigham Young's time," he burst out.

While placing Dr. Talmage as a contemporary of the second President of the Church is probably a misconception not widely shared, the incident does illustrate the manner in which James E. Talmage has become more a legend than a person to a generation born only a few years after his own lifetime, but which knows him only through his writings.

Actually, Dr. Talmage was very much a "real person," a man of warmth and vitality, intensely alive and possessing a boundless store of basic humanity.

He did have an intense dedication to his work that tends to set him apart from the common mold. In his later years he had no recreational interests in the conventional sense, no sports or games or hobbies that were not closely associated with his work. His work *was* his recreation. Even in his youth, James' participation in sports was rare, although he did enjoy fishing and returned to it with nostalgic enjoyment on occasions later in life. But he never took time to indulge this hobby extensively, or to acquire the advanced skills of the scientific angler, although he could admire these in other people.

In his boyhood, wildfowling with his grandfather had been one of James' keenest pleasures, and shotgunning remained one of his few recreational indulgences for some years after he came to America. As the years advanced, however, he developed an increasing aversion to the unnecessary taking of life, and lost his love of shooting. He would hunt game for food when it was needed, on his various expeditions through the deserts and mountains of Southern Utah, but after reaching maturity it is doubtful that he ever again shot game solely for sport.

In later years, James' long hours of work, unrelieved by periods of recreation, were cause for real concern among family, friends, and associates. President Heber J. Grant, for one, repeatedly urged Dr. Talmage to take up some form of sport, if only for its therapeutic value. Himself an enthusiastic golfer, President Grant tried to get his friend to try that sport, confident (as are all golfers) that if anyone were once thoroughly exposed to golf he would be captivated by its subtle but powerful attractions.

As President Grant's urgings increased in frequency and intensity, so did Dr. Talmage's demurrers on the grounds of lack of interest and lack of ability to master a complicated skill so late in life. President Grant was certain the skill could be mastered and that interest would automatically follow. Finally a compromise was reached, and a test agreed upon: James would give the game of golf an honest trial, and work at it until he was able to hit a drive which President Grant would rate as satisfactory, "a real golf shot."

"If you hit just one really good drive, nature will do the rest," President Grant assured his pupil-to-be. "You won't be able to resist the game after that."

It was agreed that James would make his own choice after he had acquired the skill to hit the specified shot. If he felt the fascination of the game, as President Grant was certain he would, he would take up golf and play with reasonable regularity. If, after giving the game a fair trial, James still felt no interest, President Grant would cease his efforts to get Dr. Talmage to play.

On an appointed day, the two, accompanied by a number of others of the General Authorities who played golf and who had joined the friendly argument on the side of President Grant, proceeded to Nibley Park for James' first session in what was expected to be a series of lessons.

James removed his coat and was shown how to grip the club and take his stance at the ball. The coordinated movements involved in making a golf stroke were carefully explained and then demonstrated by President Grant and by others. Finally it came James' turn to try it himself.

What followed astonished all those who watched, and probably James himself. Instead of missing the ball completely, or weakly pushing it a few feet along the grass, James somehow managed to strike the ball cleanly and with substantial force. It took off in a fine arc and with only a minimum amount of slice. Some who saw it described it later as "a truly magnificent drive," which was probably a considerable exaggeration. However, there was consensus that the ball went close to 200 yards and stayed in the fairway. It was a drive that would have gladdened the heart of any golfer short of the expert class, and it bordered on the phenomenal for a novice.

The spectators were momentarily struck dumb, then burst into enthusiastic applause.

"Congratulations," said President Grant, rushing forward, beaming, with outstretched hand. "That was a fine shot you will remember for the rest of your life."

"You mean *that* was a fully satisfactory golf shot?" James asked, cautiously.

"It certainly was!" said President Grant.

"Then I have fulfilled my part of the agreement?"

"You have—and don't you feel the thrill of excitement? Now you'll be playing regularly. As a matter of fact, we can go into the clubhouse now and I will help you select a set of clubs."

"Thank you," said James, putting on his coat. "If I have carried out my part of the agreement, then I shall call on you to live up to yours. You promised that if I hit a satis-factory drive and did not feel the spontaneous desire to play, you would stop urging me to do so. Now I should like to get back to the office, where I have a great deal of work waiting."

So far as is known, James never again struck a golf ball, or made the attempt.

While Dr. Talmage lacked interest in formal sports or games, he was anything but an ivory tower recluse, living in a world apart from the physical realities of life. His relatively small body—five feet nine inches in height and weighing around 150 pounds in his prime—was rugged and rawhide tough, as he proved on his extensive wilderness expeditions. His horsemanship was more than adequate and he rode with assurance on any type of mount from a well-bred, thoroughly-trained saddle horse to an unbroken desert mustang, as he had to do on more than one emergency occasion.

James' physical tastes and habits were extremely simple, bordering on the ascetic, yet he developed a keen appreciation for many of the refinements of civilized living. His extensive travels made him acquainted with the cooking of many lands and he took delight in fine food on occasion. He sometimes jokingly described himself as a *gourmet,* taking care to dis-tinguish the *gourmet* (one who appreciates fine quality in food) from the *gourmand* (who consumes it in excessive quantity). He did have some of the qualities of a trained palate and appreciation for subtle flavors of the *gourmet,* but no one who saw his normal eating habits, which were of the simplest, would ever confuse him with the true *gourmet,* to whom eating is one of the major concerns of life.

Intellectually as well as physically, James' tastes were keen and refined—and, because of the press of work, rarely indulged. All his life he enjoyed the theater, which he attended when he could, both when at home and on his travels. He saw many of the great dramatic performers of his day, includ-ing such legends of the theater as Sir Henry Irving, Edwin Booth, and the great Sarah Bernhardt, whose ability to project, in Rostand's *L'Aiglon,* the full image of an 18-year-old boy when she was a crippled woman of 76, drew James' amazed admiration. Yet in later years, James generally preferred to *read* great plays rather than see them performed on the stage. He pointed out that "every character emerges clearly as I picture him or her, and not as the creation of some performer whose concept may be different than mine, and who comes constantly between me and the author."

Seen only through the medium of his writings on theology, Dr. Talmage may appear as a somewhat stern and always serious-minded man, but in life he was not only warm and understanding but also possessed of a rich sense of humor. He enjoyed a good story and was himself an accomplished story teller. He had a keen wit which normally was gentle and kindly, most considerate of the feelings of others. When the occasion demanded, however, it could be surgically sharp and it was always surgically clean.

James had an unquenchable thirst for knowledge and the teacher's zeal to impart it to others. In this respect particularly, the influence of Karl G. Maeser was manifest in James E. Talmage throughout his life.

As an educator, Dr. Talmage was very much a man for his time and for the conditions in which he lived. His major concern in the field of education was to help build a sound, adequate system of teaching in his chosen field, the physical sciences, for the people of Utah who were in the 1880's still somewhat remote from the established centers of learning.

From earliest pioneer days, Utahns had been particularly concerned with education, and this interest has continued to the present day, but the early schools had been of pioneer simplicity. Many advanced areas of learning, notably the physical sciences, were of necessity badly neglected in the early days of settlement and the decades which immediately followed. There had been men of learning and ability in the field of physical science among the pioneers of 1847 and those who came immediately afterward. For the most part, however, their knowledge and abilities were fully occupied in the practical and critical tasks of carving cities out of the wilderness, building a stable economy, and meeting the myriad day-to-day problems that are part and parcel of colonization. James E. Talmage, although coming on the scene some decades after the first pioneer settlement, was a pioneer in Utah education, particularly in his chosen field of study.

Much of his teaching was of elemental simplicity, even in the light of the more limited knowledge of his day, but this was by design. It opened the eyes of a generation of Utahns to the fascinating world of scientific knowledge and showed them the paths that stretched out ahead with no visible end. James helped untold numbers to start down these paths and to go considerable distances along them. He opened the way for other educators to follow and pursue further.

His personal education James looked upon as a means to an end, never as an end in itself. He described it more than once as comparable to a bee going out to find honey and bringing it back to the hive. In accordance with counsel which he sought and received from the President of the Church, James made the seeking of academic degrees and honors secondary to his basic purpose of acquiring knowledge and using it for the good of others. Recognition and marks of distinction in the worlds of scholarship and of science did come to him, as had been promised in the special blessings pronounced upon him, but on most occasions he was extremely modest about displaying them. The exceptions came when he was appearing as a representative of the Church in places where the Mormons were considered a coarse or backward people. Then he might make the fullest use of his worldly honors and titles, and he did so with great success in the lecture tour in Britain in 1898, in many of his special lecture appearances at major universities and before philosophical and scientific societies in the United States, and in the successful campaign to eliminate the flood of anti-Mormon lies from the British press in the 1920's.

The power of Dr. Talmage's pen lives on in his published works and is felt by succeeding generations. But the power of his eloquence was something which only those who heard him speak could fully appreciate. He himself had a marked distaste for the designation "orator," with its implications of artifice and trickery in vocal persuasion, and he frequently protested the application of this title to himself. Yet it is unquestionable that Dr. Talmage *was* a most accomplished orator in the highest sense of the term. There was no artifice or deception in his presentations from the pulpit, but his command of the language, his profound knowledge of the subjects on which he spoke, and the vibrant intensity of his sincerity were electrifying and carried conviction to audiences of widely differing backgrounds in many parts of the world.

In the days before electronic amplification, Dr. Talmage's resonant voice carried with unusual effectiveness to the largest audiences. In later years when the microphone became a standard feature of the speaker's podium, he adapted to the new medium and projected the nuances of vocal emphasis in restrained volume that was suited to public address systems and to radio broadcasting.

One of the questions most frequently asked about James E. Talmage was how he could achieve such distinction as he did, both as a man of science and as a theologian, and how he reconciled the conflicts between science and religion.

Probably the simplest and most direct answer to that question is that he did not believe there was, or is, any genuine conflict, and he did not concern himself excessively over superficial differences that he was confident would be resolved with time and the acquisition of greater knowledge and enlightenment.

Over the years, James came more and more to the conclusion that much of the science-religion controversy was based on violent arguments from both sides that were directed against false targets—misconceptions or deliberate distortions of the positions taken by those on the other side. James himself was able to see an ever-growing volume of evidence supporting belief in the existence and supreme power of God, and of the recorded scriptures, in the investigations of science. In an address given in the Salt Lake Tabernacle, he said:

We are told that scientists and theologians are at hopeless and irreconcilable variance. I regard [this] . . . as an exaggeration.

Discrepancies that trouble us now will diminish as our knowledge of pertinent facts is extended. The Creator has made a record in the rocks for man to decipher; but He has also spoken directly regarding the main stages of progress by which the earth has been brought to be what it is. The accounts cannot be fundamentally opposed; one cannot contradict the other; though man's interpretation of either may be seriously at fault.

Regarding the theories evolved by scientific researchers to account for various phenomena they observed, James said:

Theories may be regarded as the scaffolding upon which the builder stands while placing the blocks of truth in position. It is a grave error to mistake the scaffolding for the wall, the flimsy temporary structure for the stable and permanent. . . . Theories have their purpose and are indispensable, but they must never be mistaken for demonstrated facts.

On the other hand, Dr. Talmage believed that Holy Writ should not be regarded as something other than what it was intended to be.

The opening chapters of Genesis, and scriptures related thereto, were never intended as a textbook of geology, archaeology, earth-science, or man-science. Holy Scripture will endure, while the conceptions of men change with new discoveries. We do not show reverence for the scriptures when we misapply them through faulty interpretation.

Men should concentrate on fundamentals, not lose themselves in arguments over details and superficialities, James sincerely believed. That God created the earth and all that is in it, is fundamental: whether or not a man or woman believes this determines that person's whole approach to life. Precisely *how* the Lord accomplished the work of creation is something that has never been fully and in detail revealed, either by direct word of the Lord or through the investigations of men. Until the Almighty does provide man with detailed knowledge, it is worse than useless to argue details that are based on theories or partial knowledge, although it is proper for men to use their God-given intelligence to seek for truth in the evidences of nature.

> The scientist is busily engaged in the study of secondary causes —the ways and means by which God works and through which He accomplishes His miracle. The Holy Scriptures should not be discredited by theories of men; they cannot be discredited by fact and truth.
>
> Within the Gospel of Jesus Christ there is room and place for every truth thus far learned by man, or yet to be made known.

Thus was the matter summed up by Dr. Talmage—Educator, Scientist, Apostle.

CHAPTER

TWENTY-THREE

# Final Curtain

On the evening of Sunday, July 23, 1933, James E. Talmage delivered his scheduled talk over KSL at the appointed time and in the long-familiar routine. Son-in-law Harold Brandley filled his customary role of chauffeur and special helper, assisting Dr. Talmage to descend the back stairs from the Church Office Building and to get in and out of the car and of the old Deseret News Building at South Temple and Main Streets which housed the KSL studios.

After the broadcast, James suggested a detour to the A & W Root Beer drive-in establishment at Fifth South and State Streets for refreshment before returning to the office. This was prompted not only by the hot, muggy night, which made the thought of a cooling drink appealing, but also because James had been bothered throughout the evening by a persistent tickling in his throat that coughing could not seem to reach. The sting of the root beer's carbonation brought welcome relief, and James indulged in a second glass as he and Harold sat and chatted pleasantly of many things, including the seven delightful Brandley girls who were so dear to their grandfather's heart.

By the time they returned to the Church Office Building, Dr. Talmage felt greatly refreshed, and much relieved from the annoying throat irritation which had been bothering him. Harold saw James safely ensconced in his office, checked that his needs were provided for, and left with the mutual understanding that Dr. Talmage would remain in the office over the morrow's Pioneer Day holiday.

James slept fitfully on the couch in the office, for the tickling in his throat returned persistently. Cough drops brought only temporary relief, and by morning the mild tickling had a painful irritation. In addition, he had the beginnings of a headache and a feeling of vague uneasiness all over his body.

James knew he was ill, but did not want to upset the holiday plans of those at home. The other offices were empty in deference to "the Twenty-Fourth," and James decided to wait until the return to normal routines on the next day before having his physical condition checked. He tried to immerse himself in work as a means of forgetting his discomfort, as he had many times done in the past, lay down for prolonged spells on the couch, and from time to time listened by radio to accounts of the Pioneer Day activities.

Monday night passed restlessly, as sleep was fitful, but dreams drifted in and out of James' consciousness in a most confusing way. The pain in his throat and his headache increased in intensity.

By Tuesday morning, there was no doubt that James was seriously ill. His head was alarmingly hot and throbbed steadily. His mouth was dry and his throat acutely painful. He called home and asked to be picked up. When aid arrived, James was so weak that he had to be carried from the building. He was taken home—to the old family residence at 304 First Avenue to which he and Maia had returned—and put to bed and a doctor was summoned. The doctor found James to be suffering from a severe streptococcus infection.

Within two years, the remarkable effectiveness of the sulpha drugs in controlling "strep" infections would be known, and within a decade penicillin would be discovered, to dominate the streptococcus bacilli even more effectively than the sulphas. But this was 1933, and a "strep throat" was not a routine minor ailment almost certain to respond to proper treatment, but a deeply dreaded threat to life. It was to be eradicated in its early stages, for if it once got established in the patient's blood stream, chances of arresting it were meagre. The long hours over the holiday when Dr. Talmage had been without medical attention had allowed the dread infection to become thoroughly established in his system.

Throughout Wednesday, James tossed in delirium while every known remedy was applied. Maia stayed constantly at his bedside, assisted by those of the children who were at home. The doctor came at frequent intervals. The Priesthood, of course, was called to administer to James, but the feeling was strong that the appointed end of his earthly mission might be fast approaching.

By Wednesday night, if there was no visible improvement in James' condition, at least he seemed to be holding his own. The doctor reported to May that James' heart was still "strong and sound as that of a young man," and the heart was the critical point where the dread streptococcus concentrated its attack.

Thursday morning, July 27, was calm and still, not a breath of wind rustling the leaves on the trees. The cool of the night had not yet started to give way to the oppressive heat of the day as May stood at the window of the room where James lay stricken, watching the misty gray of the sky turn rosy-pink, then slowly change to pale blue which gradually gained in depth of color until it showed the pure azure of the summer day. A desperate prayer was in her heart, but gradually it was replaced by a deep peace. She knew the end was near, yet for a few moments the anguish and immense sense of loss she would know were set aside by the feelings of love and gratitude for all the wonderful years that had been.

When the doctor arrived, he found that a startling change had taken place in his patient. The heart, which only a few hours previously had been strong and sound as that of a young man, had almost disintegrated under the assault of the streptococcus bacilli and gave only a wild, disorganized, fluttery beat. There was no longer any hope of recovery, and the time remaining was measured not in days or hours but in minutes.

At 8:45 A.M. James E. Talmage had passed away. The immediate cause of death was officially recorded as "acute myocarditis, following a throat infection."

At his bedside when the end came were Maia, dry-eyed and numb from the impact of a blow whose full effect was too great to be realized at once and would be absorbed over the lonely years ahead; son Paul; two of the three living daughters, Elsie and Helen; Elsie's husband Harold; and Dr. Talmage's long-time friend and associate, J. Reuben Clark, Jr. Sterling was en route from New Mexico, Lucile from California, and Karl from the Pacific Northwest. John was in far-off France, just preparing to sail for home after three years in the mission field.

The *Deseret News* that evening carried a headline in inch-high block capital letters across the full width of the front page, proclaiming the stark message:

## DOCTOR JAMES E. TALMAGE IS DEAD

The First Presidency, the Council of the Twelve of which he had been a member for more than a score of years, the First Council of Seventy, the Presiding Bishopric, and a number of close personal friends and associates issued statements paying tribute to Dr. Talmage for his many and varied accomplishments and for his humanity.

The *Salt Lake Tribune,* voice of the "Gentile" element in the community, the *Tribune* which in past years—under different ownership and very different editorial policy—had often vitriolically attacked him and his public sermons, had this to say of Dr. Talmage:

> . . . No creed, no group, no individual, appreciative of the value of public service and cognizant of the sterling character and ability of this man, is spared a portion of the widespread grief attending the departure of Dr. Talmage for the realm of the unknown.
>
> This forceful personality left a mark in local history which must remain, not alone for sentimental reasons, but for meritorious

contribution to humanity. His life was devoted to accomplishment. . . . Few have equalled him as a champion of the L.D.S.
faith. It is not ungrateful to others to say that none have surpassed him in the period during which he lived as an exponent of
Mormon theology.

In the field of public service, beyond the scope of religious
activity, this esteemed and respected character attained national
and international recognition. He commanded attention as a scientist, an educator, and as a writer. He was a fellow of numerous
societies, and the author of many theological works. As a public
speaker, particularly from the pulpit, he displayed an amazing
breadth of knowledge, an imbedded sympathy for his fellow-man,
and a degree of tolerance which profoundly impressed and influenced his audiences.

The record of deeds well done left by Dr. Talmage eases the
pain of the final parting with one who not only assisted in the
struggle of life, but pointed out the way. . . .

The funeral was held on Sunday, July 30, in the Tabernacle where James, in the vigor of life, had so often and so
effectively occupied the pulpit. The great edifice was filled,
the areas behind the speaker's pulpit banked with flowers.
The majestic Tabernacle organ played Handel's *Largo* as the
family walked in to take their places. (Over the ensuing
eleven years while she patiently awaited the blessed moment
when she could rejoin her beloved husband, Maia would never
hear those strains without their bringing back the whole scene
with a vivid intensity that was almost overwhelming.) All
of the living members of the family except John were home
for the funeral.

Members of the Council of the Twelve were honorary
pallbearers. Active pallbearers were chosen from the ranks
of the splendid young men, so much loved and admired by
Dr. Talmage in life, who had served with him at European
Mission headquarters: Richard L. Evans, Ralph Chisholm,
Seth W. Pixton, James M. Armstrong, Rulon Sanders, and
Junius S. Romney.

Speakers at the services were Melvin J. Ballard and

This rough-hewn granite monument stands over the final resting-place of James E. Talmage's mortal remains in the Salt Lake City Cemetery. The dark spot in the upper center section of the granite is not for decorative effect, but is a xenolith with special geological significance.

President Rudger Clawson of the Council of the Twelve, and all three members of the First Presidency: J. Reuben Clark, Jr., Anthony W. Ivins, and Heber J. Grant.

Perhaps the essence of their combined talks was expressed by President Ivins when he said:

> There will never be any other man to take his place, so far as I am concerned. There may be other men just as good, there may be other men just as wise, but his particular place in the Church and in the lives of those with whom he came in contact, will never be filled again until we meet him.

James E. Talmage was laid to rest in the family plot in the city cemetery which for nearly forty years tiny Zella had occupied alone. A simple monument was placed over his grave, of Utah granite rough-hewn to preserve the rugged, natural look, similar to those which James had observed in Finland and of which he had many times spoken to his family.

Centered near the top of the face of the stone is a xenolith, or "rock within a rock," a piece of darker sedimentary limestone which was engulfed in the igneous granite when it was still molten in a long-past geological age. The xenolith is not there by chance, nor was the stone containing it selected for its decorative effect. It symbolized a contribution of Dr. Talmage, the geologist. It had earlier been thought that the Utah granite was older than the nearby sedimentary rocks. Dr. Talmage's observation of the numerous xenoliths and the deduction that the limestone must have existed while the granite was still in a molten state was instrumental in fixing the Utah rock formations in their proper places in the geological tables.

The smoothed portion of the face of the monument carries the simple inscription:

*James E. Talmage*

*Educator    Scientist    Apostle*

and a brief quotation from his writings which, perhaps as well as any other single sentence, catches the essence of his philosophy:

"Within the Gospel of Jesus Christ there is room and place for every truth thus far learned by man, or yet to be made known."

# Appendix

Ancestors of James E. Talmage, and Descendants as
of January, 1972

Talmage, William, md. 1595 to Blake, Alice
  Talmage, John, b. 1603, md. Reanes, Joane, 1628
    Talmage, John, b. 1642, md. Sloper, Elizabeth, 1667
      Talmage, Roger, b. 1672, md. Davis, Hannah, 1697
        Talmage, Robert, b. 1699, md. Hine, Anne, 1727
          Talmage, William, b. 1731, md. Cox, Mary, 1773
            Talmage, James, b. 1774, md. Piper, Martha, 1799
              Talmage, James, b. 1799, md. Joyce, Mary
                Talmage, James Joyce, b. 1840, md. Preater, Susannah, 1860

TALMAGE, JAMES EDWARD, b. Sept. 21, 1862
md. Merry May Booth, June 14, 1888

| Sterling | Paul | Zella | Elsie | James | Lucile | Helen | John |
| Booth | Booth | | | Karl | | May | Russell |

*Sterling Booth Talmage,* b. May 21, 1889; md. Nelle Allen, Nov. 13, 1912.
No issue. Died Nov. 8, 1956.

*Paul Booth Talmage,* b. Dec. 21, 1891; md. Edna Marie Turner, July 18, 1917;
md. Etsa Johnson Miller, April 1, 1933.
  Phyllis Jane, b. March 2, 1919.
  *Phyllis Jane Talmage,* md. Arthur Mortensen, April 9, 1943.
    David, b. April 5, 1947; Jane, b. Sept. 30, 1949; Mary, b. Jan. 21, 1952;
    Ellen, b. April 20, 1953.

*Zella Talmage,* b. Aug. 3, 1894. Died in infancy, April 27, 1895.

*Elsie Talmage,* b. August 16, 1896; md. Harold C. Brandley, Sept. 12, 1917.
  Barbara and Elizabeth (twins), b. Sept. 22, 1918; Norma Deane, b. March 18,
  1920; Joyce, b. Oct. 30, 1922; Helen, b. March 8, 1924, Susanne Jean, b. June
  17, 1926; Rosemary, b. April 14, 1931.
  *Barbara Brandley,* md. Norman Steed Howells, June 30, 1941.
    Michele, b. March 24, 1943; Marsha, b. July 28, 1945; Shannon, b. Aug. 18,
    1947; Pamela, b. Aug. 20, 1949; Lynne, b. July 15, 1952; Candyce, b. Oct.
    11, 1953.
    *Marsha Howells,* md. Michael James Donahoo.
    Michael Norman, Janelle.
  *Elizabeth Brandley,* md. William F. Schultz, Feb. 11, 1942.
    Stephen Douglas, b. June 17, 1943; Stephanie, b. June 8, 1946; John Wil-
    liam, b. April 14, 1948; Gregory, b. July 7, 1954.
    *Stephen Douglas Schultz,* md. Connie Peterson.
    Stephen Matthew.
    *Stephanie Schultz,* md. William Harley English.
    Joshua William, Jeremy.
    *John William Schultz,* md. Susan Ray Allred.
    Kimberly.

*Norma Deane Brandley,* md. William L. Troxler, Jan. 1, 1942.
Susan, b. April 23, 1943; Joel, b. Aug. 6, 1946; Julie, b. March 26, 1951;
Kathleen, b. Aug. 5, 1952.
*Susan Troxler,* md. George Douglas Holt.
Talmage, Jeffrey William.
*Joel Troxler,* md. Beverly Guster.
Ian Joel.

*Joyce Brandley,* md. Robert L. Johnson, Dec. 5, 1945.
Marc Brandley, b. May 20, 1947; Jeffrey Lander, b. Jan. 3, 1949; Jane, b.
March 19, 1951; Richard Linn, b. April 17, 1956; Robert Lander, b. April
25, 1958.

*Helen Brandley,* md. Wayne Wiscomb, June 12, 1942.
Brenda Lee, b. Sept. 22, 1943; Chrisanne, b. March 9, 1948; Allison, b. Jan.
11, 1950; Brett, b. Aug. 8, 1952; Wayne, Jr., b. Jan. 31, 1954; Jenifer, b.
Dec. 27, 1956; Amy Rebecca, b. March 2, 1961.
*Brenda Lee Wiscomb,* md. Peter M. Lowe, Jr.
David Eric, Michael, Evan Peter, Chelsi Eliza.

*Susanne Jean Brandley,* md. Robert M. Winston, Oct. 12, 1944.
Jeffrey Talmage, b. July 15, 1945; Harold Michael, b. March 19, 1948;
David DeShon, b. Sept. 21, 1950; Susanne, b. March 21, 1954.

*Rosemary Brandley,* md. Rex. W. Williams, Aug. 10, 1950.
Becky, b. May 26, 1951; Brooke Spencer, b. April 26, 1952; Rex Brandley,
b. Feb. 3, 1954; Thomas Brandley, b. Aug. 1, 1961.

*James Karl Talmage,* b. Aug. 29, 1898; md. Maybelle Gurrad, 1922.
James K., b. Aug. 14, 1923.
*James K. Talmage,* md. Joanne Abrahmson, April 29, 1947.
David Paul, b. Nov. 26, 1948; Christine Lynn, b. Nov. 14, 1950.
*James K. Talmage,* md. Barbara Ann Carothers, Nov. 20, 1959.
Elizabeth Karen, b. April 13, 1964; James Michael, b. Aug. 5, 1968.

*Lucile Talmage,* b. May 29, 1900; md. Wilford C. Carlisle, April 14, 1920.
Richard Talmage, b. Dec. 7, 1920; Joan Patrice, b. July 15, 1925.

*Richard Talmage Carlisle,* md. Evelyn Estrella Lauber, Feb. 6, 1944.
Kristen, b. Nov. 18, 1947; Donald Talmage, b. May 19, 1952.

*Joan Patrice Carlisle,* md. James Orson Douglas, April 18, 1943.
Anne, b. Dec. 30, 1943; James Orson, Jr., b. May 11, 1950; David Carlisle,
b. May 30, 1955; Susan, b. Jan. 22, 1962.
*Anne Douglas,* md. Charles L. Dreilinger, March 21, 1966.
Sean Eric, Seth Aaron, Daniel Ethan.
*James Orson Douglas, Jr.,* md. Connie Rae Carver, Jan. 21, 1970.
James Jason.

*Helen May Talmage,* b. Oct. 24, 1902; md. Roland Parry, April 2, 1926.
Gloria, b. July 6, 1927; James Talmage, b. Sept. 30, 1928.

*Gloria Parry,* md. Bruce A. Walter, Feb. 4, 1956.
Maia Marion, b. Jan. 7, 1957; Wendy Diane, b. July 24, 1958; Shelley
Kathleen, b. Oct. 17, 1959; Allison Ann, b. Aug. 8, 1965.

*James Talmage Parry,* md. Carol Dunn, Jan. 9, 1951.
Susan, b. Dec. 16, 1951; Rosemary, b. May 4, 1960.

*John Russell Talmage,* b. Feb. 1, 1911; md. Mary Merrell Jones, Dec. 20, 1935
(died childless); md. Virginia Graves Noehren, Nov. 1, 1945.
James Arthur, b. March 13, 1948; Carol Jeanne, b. March 23, 1950; Mary
Alison, b. June 27, 1953; Robert Sterling, b. Oct. 17, 1955; Roger Edward, b.
April 1, 1957.

# Index